50 Walks and Hikes in
Banff National Park

Summerthought
Banff, Alberta

Published by

Summerthought

Summerthought Publishing
PO Box 2309
Banff, AB   T1L 1C1
Canada
www.summerthought.com

Printing History
1st Edition—2008

Library and Archives Canada Cataloguing in Publication

Patton, Brian, 1943-
50 Walks and Hikes in Banff National Park / Brian Patton and Bart Robinson.

Includes bibliographical references and index.

ISBN 978-0-9782375-3-0

1. Hiking—Alberta—Banff National Park—Guidebooks. 2. Walking—Alberta—Banff National Park—Guidebooks. 3. Trails—Alberta—Banff National Park—Guidebooks. 4. Banff National Park (Alta.)—Guidebooks. I. Robinson, Bart II. Title. III. Title: 50 Walks and Hikes in Banff National Park.

FC3664.B3P38 2008   796.522097123'32   C2007-906891-X

All photos copyright © 2008 Brian Patton or Andrew Hempstead except: copyright © Whyte Museum of the Canadian Rockies (V633-NA-1796), page 22; © Whyte Museum of the Canadian Rockies (V48 NA65 226), page 30; copyright © Shadow Lake Lodge, page 84; copyright © Paula Worthington, page 113.

Front cover photo: Lake Louise Shoreline Trail. © Andrew Hempstead/www.heejee.com
Back cover photo: Lower Consolation Lake. © Andrew Hempstead/www.heejee.com
Design and production: Linda Petras
Printed in Canada by Friesens

50 Walks and Hikes in
Banff National Park

Brian Patton *and* Bart Robinson

Summerthought
Banff, Alberta

Table of Contents

LAKE LOUISE/MORAINE LAKE — 87

ICEFIELDS PARKWAY — 119

Preface

When we set out to write the first edition of the *Canadian Rockies Trail Guide* in 1970, the hiking trails of Banff National Park were the ones we knew best and were the inspiration for our book covering all of the Canadian Rockies. We'd hiked enough at that point in our young lives to know that this park contained more great short hikes and day trips than any similar area in North America.

While our initial plan to publish a trail guide to Banff National Park was soon replaced by the more grandiose *Canadian Rockies Trail Guide,* we knew the section on Banff would be the most-used chapter. In addition to being Canada's most-visited national park, it contains more than 1,500 kilometres (930 miles) of trail, much of which is devoted to walks and short hikes that can be completed in a day or less. More than 20 of these trips include lakes along the way or as a primary destination—a big plus for most hikers. Other trails lead to high viewpoints overlooking rugged, glaciated peaks or into the treeless alpine zone. And all of the trails display a variety of wildflowers and wildlife throughout the hiking season.

So, many years after originally planning a guidebook dedicated to Banff, we have created *50 Walks and Hikes in Banff National Park.* This book contains more elements of value to the walker and day-hiker than the *Canadian Rockies Trail Guide,* including useful and interesting facts about each trail, colour topographical maps, and colour photographs. Most importantly, for us personally, this book is an opportunity to highlight the trails that have been a special part of our lives for almost four decades. There isn't a single trail in this book that we haven't hiked on numerous occasions and at all the months of the hiking season. We hope you receive as much pleasure from these trips as we have.

Brian Patton and Bart Robinson

Acknowledgements

This book would not exist without the vision and energy of Summerthought publisher Andrew Hempstead, who guided the project from beginning to end, hiked most of the trails and provided much of the photography. As she has in the past, Linda Petras helped create a design for the book that is both useful and attractive.

We would also like to thank the people who have kept us up-to-date on the trails and parks backcountry policy in Banff National Park over the years, and most recently Jenny Klafki of Parks Canada and Joel Hagen and Nadine Fletcher of Great Divide Nature Interpretation.

About the Authors

For the past 35 years, Brian Patton has interpreted the natural and human history of the Canadian Rockies in books, on film and through presentations. His other books include the *Canadian Rockies Trail Guide, Parkways of the Canadian Rockies, Tales from the Canadian Rockies, Mountain Chronicles: Jon Whyte* and *Bear Tales from the Canadian Rockies.* He continues to work on a variety projects from his home in Invermere, British Columbia.

Following the publication of the *Canadian Rockies Trail Guide,* Bart Robinson authored several books on the Canadian Rockies: *Banff Springs: The Story of a Hotel, Columbia Icefield: A Solitude of Ice* and *Great Days in the Rockies: The Photographs of Byron Harmon.* Subsequently, he has enjoyed a long career as a journalist, editor, and conservationist. He currently lives in Canmore, Alberta.

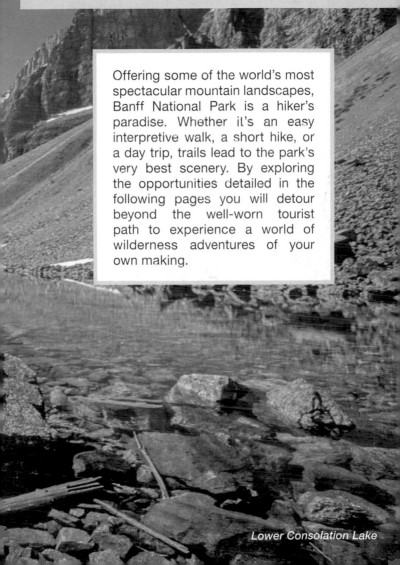

Introduction

Offering some of the world's most spectacular mountain landscapes, Banff National Park is a hiker's paradise. Whether it's an easy interpretive walk, a short hike, or a day trip, trails lead to the park's very best scenery. By exploring the opportunities detailed in the following pages you will detour beyond the well-worn tourist path to experience a world of wilderness adventures of your own making.

Lower Consolation Lake

Using This Book

The Regions

The trails in *50 Walks and Hikes in Banff National Park* are organized by the following regions:

Town of Banff: The town of Banff lies in the south of the park, a 90-minute drive west of Calgary. Some trails can be accessed on foot from downtown while others, such as those along Lake Minnewanka Road, require a vehicle or bike to access.

Banff to Lake Louise: The Trans-Canada Highway takes 56 kilometers (35 miles) to reach Lake Louise from Banff, while the Bow Valley Parkway is a little longer. Trails in this chapter begin along both these roads.

Lake Louise/Moraine Lake: Banff National Park's two most famous lakes provide the starting point for some of the oldest and most scenic recreational trails in the Canadian Rockies.

Icefields Parkway: This scenically famous highway winds its way north from Lake Louise to Jasper National Park. The first 122 kilometers (76 miles) parallel the Continental Divide to the northern boundary of Banff National Park.

Trail Summary

The introductory information for each walk and hike will help you decide if it is appropriate for your ability and how much time you have. It includes the following elements:

Length: Whenever a trail runs out and back on the same route, distances quoted are one-way. But for loop trips (circuits), total distance is provided.

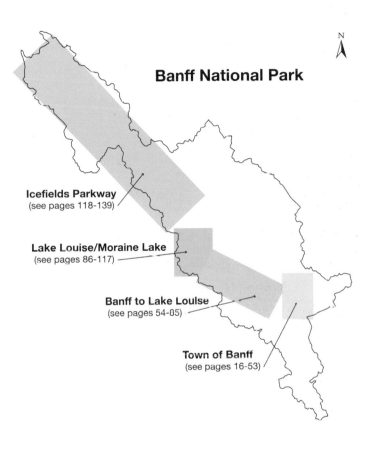

N

Banff National Park

Icefields Parkway
(see pages 118-139)

Lake Louise/Moraine Lake
(see pages 86-117)

Banff to Lake Louise
(see pages 54-85)

Town of Banff
(see pages 16-53)

Elevation gain: This is the total ascent, in metres (m) and feet (ft), over the one-way course of the trail; if there is a significant loss of elevation, it is also noted.

Walking time: The length of time it will take to reach your objective. In the case of loop trips, total time is presented. Anyone of moderate fitness can complete the trails in the time allotted. Strong hikers will need less time, but if you stop for lunch or frequent breaks it will take you a little longer.

Starting point: Directions for reaching the trailhead

Origin of the name: Most place names in Banff National Park describe a natural feature or recognize early explorers and their peers.

Trail Designations

The hiking trails in Banff National Park vary greatly in length and difficulty. In this book, rather than designate a difficulty factor, we have applied the following terms:

EASY WALK: Usually less than one hour and with minimal elevation gain.

SHORT HIKE: Elevation gain varies, but these trails can be completed in three hours or less.

DAY TRIP: A day trip doesn't necessarily mean you'll spend a full day hiking, but rather, at least four hours.

OVERNIGHT: This book purposely ignores hiking trails that require camping in the backcountry, but the two overnight trips we do include offer the luxury of staying in remote lodges while hiking with just a light pack.

Most trails in Banff National Park are well signposted.

Symbols

The following symbols are used to illustrate services and facilities associated with each trail:

- The trail is signposted from the highway
- A covered kiosk with a map and trail conditions at the trailhead
- Picnic tables at the trailhead
- Washrooms at the trailhead
- Food services, such as a café, are within walking distance of the trailhead
- Bicycles are allowed on the trail
- While they may be snow-covered, these trails can be walked year-round.

Weather

Despite the northerly latitude of the range, the Canadian Rockies experience climate and weather patterns that compare closely with higher mountain ranges further the south. For example, temperature and annual precipitation in the town of Banff are very similar to those of West Yellowstone, Montana, and Leadville, Colorado.

The mountain snowpack usually begins to disappear as temperatures moderate in April. By mid-May hiking is possible on low elevation trails in the Bow Valley and on south-facing slopes. By late June most trails below treeline are snowfree, but many are still wet and muddy. Above treeline, trails open from early July to early August, depending on slope exposure, snowpack and weather.

Mid-July to mid-August is considered peak hiking season. During this period, the warmest weeks of summer are experienced, there is usually less rainfall than spring, and alpine wildflowers are in bloom. Of course, this is also when trails are most heavily used.

The Banff Visitor Centre is the best place to ask about weather forecasts and trail conditions.

High country temperatures start to fall in late August, and early September usually sees the first snow falling in the high country. However, these early storms are usually short-lived, and the latter weeks of September and early October are often blessed by beautiful weather (known as an Indian summer). Weather changes quickly and dramatically at this time of year, so be prepared for surprise storms and the possibility of some cold, snowy hiking.

Dangers and Annoyances

Compared to many of the world's wild regions, Banff National Park is a relatively benign area when it comes to dangerous beasts and other natural hazards. Yet there are a few creatures, both great and small, worthy of discussion.

Bears

While rare, it is a good idea to be prepared for an unexpected bear encounter and, even more importantly, to follow a few basic rules to avoid the encounter in the first place:

- Check trail reports and posted warnings at park visitor centres for a listing of trails where bears have been sighted.

- Watch for bear sign, such as fresh droppings, diggings, or tracks. If you come across an animal carcass, leave the area immediately.

Grizzly bears are identified by a distinctive hump behind their necks.

- Always stay alert. You don't want to come upon a bear suddenly at close range. You should continually scan your surroundings, and peruse the slopes and valley ahead before descending from a pass or ridge.

- Make noise in areas where bears have been seen or any prime bear habitat where visibility is limited. The occasional loud shout or whistle will alert bears to your presence. Talking loudly or singing can also be effective.

- Groups of four or more hikers have far less chance of being charged or attacked. Nearly all serious attacks in the park have occurred when a single individual encountered a bear at close range.

- Bear pepper spray has proven effective in driving away aggressive bruins, but for maximum safety each member of the hiking party should be carrying a can and it should be readily accessible.

It is beyond the scope of this book to get into all the variables that must be considered during an encounter with an aggressive bear or a bear attack. Parks Canada publishes excellent brochures covering all aspects of avoidance and what to do in an attack situation. Pick one up at a park visitor centre and read it thoroughly.

Hiking is safest in groups of four or more.

Other Mammals

Far more people are charged and injured by elk each year than by bears. Aggressive elk are most common around the town of Banff and on nearby trails since these "urbanized" animals have lost their fear of humans. Never approach elk at any time of year, but give females with young a very wide berth during the calving season (late May and early June), and the same with bulls during the mating season (late August to early October).

There are no other mammals that pose a significant threat to hikers in Banff National Park. While animals such as cougar and wolverine have fierce reputations, they are usually very shy around humans and very rarely seen.

Of course, there are records of nearly every species having charged or chomped humans at one time or another. (These include an irate mother spruce grouse that permanently scarred one of the authors.) The golden rule around wildlife: always give animals room and never harass or feed them.

Ticks and Other Insects

Wood ticks are abundant in dry, grassy areas of Banff National Park in spring (early May through late June). Although ticks in the Canadian Rockies have been free of Rocky Mountain Spotted Fever and Lyme disease (so far), they can cause a potentially fatal tick paralysis if they burrow at the base of the skull. The best precaution is to wear long pants tucked into socks or gaiters and to avoid lounging about on grassy slopes. Always check your clothing and body carefully following a spring hike. When a tick is discovered, a simple touch or gentle tug often dislodges it. If it has already burrowed into the skin, grasp it as close to the skin as possible with tweezers and pull firmly but slowly. If you can't remove it, or mouthparts remain in the skin, see a doctor.

Mosquitoes are generally less of a problem in Banff National Park than they are in the mountains and wetlands farther north. However, some summers are worse than others and certain areas are renowned for their bloodsucking hordes. Hikers do not need headnets or bug jackets, but repellent should be carried throughout the hiking season until early September.

Horseflies are another common nuisance during midsummer. Insect repellent has no effect on these large biting flies, and a heavy shirt and pants are your only protection.

Giardia

Another addition to the list of hiker miseries is *giardia lamblia,* a waterborne parasite that can cause severe and prolonged gastrointestinal distress. *Giardia* is carried by many species of animals, but the human infective strain is most frequently found in beaver. While the parasite finds its way into mountain streams and rivers through the feces of many animals, beaver are best equipped to perpetuate the parasite in wilderness water systems.

Some hikers are willing to take their chances in the upper portions of watersheds, particularly above treeline or where they feel secure there is no beaver activity or human sources of contamination. But the only way to be totally safe is to bring your own bottled water.

Theft

Vehicle break-ins in Banff National Park are rare but do occur. Vehicles left at remote trailheads, such as those along the Icefields Parkway, are particularly prone. Use common sense and don't leave any valuables in your vehicle. If possible, keep all personal belongings out of sight by leaving them in the trunk. Report break-ins or suspicious behavior to the RCMP in Banff (403/762-2226) or Lake Louise (403/522-3811).

Planning Your Trip

Unless you are simply going for a short stroll, exploring Banff National Park on foot requires some advance planning. In addition to considering the practical information included in this section, you can use this book to identify which trails suit your abilities and interests in advance of arriving.

While Banff National Park is best known for its natural beauty, the park also offers an excellent tourism infrastructure. Facilities such as accommodations, restaurants, and gas stations are concentrated in the town of Banff and the village of Lake Louise. This allows visitors to spend the day hiking through the wilderness, and then soothe sore muscles in a European-style spa, dine at an upscale restaurant, and rest their heads at a luxurious lodge. For those looking for a simpler experience, campgrounds and hostels are scattered through the park. (See *Information* under *Sources* for tourism websites.)

hikers continuing around Lake Agnes beyond the teahouse

Information and Maps

We recommend that all hikers stop by a park visitor centre before embarking on any serious hiking in Banff National Park. Located in the town of Banff and the village of Lake Louise (see *Information* under *Sources*), these centres provide current weather forecasts, reports on trail conditions and closures, and warnings concerning bear activity. They also dispense free park visitor guides and a variety of pamphlets relating to bear safety, mountain biking, fishing, and more.

While the maps in this book cover each of the trails described, they are only designed to give you a general idea of trail location, course, and surrounding topography. It's always nice to have a more detailed map along to identify natural features and to help dispel confusion. The most useful of these for day hikers are produced by Gem Trek (see *Information* under *Sources.*)

What to Pack

Even if you're planning a short walk, it is essential that you are prepared for changing weather. While the following recommendations will help you decide what to pack, the lighter you travel the more enjoyable your time in the wilderness will be.

Sturdy walking shoes or hiking boots should be at the top of your must-bring list. If you have a new pair of shoes, make sure you wear them once or twice before leaving home—just to make sure they are comfortable.

In summer, temperatures rarely drop below freezing, so you don't need a winter jacket. Instead, prepare for a variety of weather conditions (especially if visiting in spring and fall) by dressing in layers. The best clothing is made from synthetic fabrics, which draw perspiration away from the body yet repel water. A breathable rain jacket should be carried regardless of the weather forecast. A warm hat and mitts are not necessary in summer, but should be packed as a precaution for longer hikes in spring and fall.

Trekking poles significantly reduce stress on knees, especially on steep descents. They also decrease strain on feet and lower backs. While ski poles are better than nothing, serious hikers will want to invest in purpose-built telescopic, anti-shock, lightweight poles with flexible tips.

While natural sunlight is good for our health, too much can have adverse effects. This is especially relevant at higher eleva-

Trekking poles are especially beneficial on rocky trails.

tions, where the air is thinner and cleaner, and the effects of UV exposure more pronounced. Therefore, it is important to wear a wide-brimmed hat and sunglasses, and to apply sunscreen, even if the temperature is not particularly high.

It is essential to keep hydrated when hiking, especially at higher elevations. Due to the possible presence of *giardia* (see *Dangers and Annoyances,* above), do not drink from mountain water sources. Instead, bring bottled water.

The walks and hikes detailed in this book do not require any special dietary considerations, although on longer walks it is important to keep your energy level up by eating high-octane carbohydrates, such as those found in energy bars. Make your hike more memorable by

A picnic always tastes better in the backcountry.

being creative when it comes to food. Pack a picnic lunch, with ingredients sourced from local stores such as Wild Flour (211 Bear St., Banff) and Laggan's (Samson Mall, Lake Louise) for bakery items, and the General Store (211 Bear St., Banff) for gourmet meats and cheeses. Remember to pack all garbage out. Do not leave anything behind—even apple cores.

Bug spray is a summer necessity. You can pick up the brands that are most effective at outdoor retailers and convenience stores throughout the park. A pre-packaged first aid kit can come in handy for those planning longer hikes, but is not necessary for short walks. Even if you don't carry a complete kit, blister moleskin (available at most drugstores) or band-aids should be carried at all times. A spare plastic bag is handy for packing out garbage.

Carry everything in a lightweight daypack, which is slung over your shoulders like a backpack. The best daypacks are durable but

Wildflower meadows are a highlight of higher elevation hikes.

lightweight, have padded shoulder straps and back panel, and are waterproof or come with a rolled up waterproof pack cover built into the base. Waterproof stuff sacks provide extra defense on rainy days.

Some Final Words

- Plan ahead. Choose trails you are in shape to handle. Allow time for unexpected weather and other events that might alter your schedule.

- Stay on the trail, even if it means muddy boots. Leaving the trail creates parallel tracks and widens existing trails. Shortcutting switchbacks causes erosion.

- Leave rocks, flowers, antlers, and other natural objects undisturbed. Never pick wildflowers or other plants.

- Never feed, disturb, or harass wildlife. It is illegal, harmful to the animal's health, and alters their natural behavior.

- Pack out all garbage. Carry plastic bags and, whenever possible, pack out litter that other, less considerate hikers have left behind.

Muddy sections don't look inviting, but stopping off the trail can cause erosion.

- Use washroom facilities provided at most trailheads.

- Give horseback parties the right-of-way. If you encounter a horseback party, step well off the trail and stand still until it has passed.

Town of Banff and Vicinity

Most park visitors base themselves in the town of Banff, a bustling community of 8,000 permanent residents located a 90-minute drive west of Calgary. Nestled in a forested valley, the town is surrounded by hiking trails—leading along the Bow River, to waterfalls, to a canyon, and ascending the surrounding mountains. Nearby are opportunities for visitors to walk back through history, explore a variety of lakes, and climb to a glacially-carved cirque.

Cascade Ponds

Bow Falls

A pleasant riverside walk

Length: 1.2 km (0.7 mi) one way
Elevation gain: minimal
Walking time: 20 minutes one way
Starting point: Central Park, corner Buffalo St. and Bow Ave.
Origin of the name: Reeds along the river were used by native people to make bows

EASY WALK

The Bow River flowing through the heart of Banff creates one of the most peaceful settings for any small town in North America. By following a trail that follows the river from the town's Central Park to Bow Falls, you can experience the best of this wonderful river and escape the hustle and bustle of downtown.

At the riverside trailhead kiosk beside the gazebo in Banff's Central Park you'll find a map showing a network of paved walking trails.

the view across to Sulphur Mountain from Central Park

The route to Bow Falls begins here and follows along the river behind the park to the Bow River Bridge.

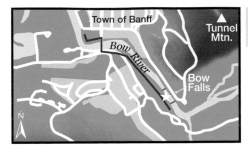

Across the river from downtown, follow the stairs leading down to the river on the downstream side of the bridge. Walk along Glen Avenue and follow the trail when it diverges from the street (look for trailhead kiosk to the left). After following the river for 500 metres (0.3 miles), it climbs a rocky outcrop, from where the first view of the falls comes into view, and then descends to a parking area and concrete pathway, from where the falls are most spectacular. The falls are most powerful in late spring, when runoff from the winter snow fills every river and stream in the Bow Valley watershed.

The falls are the result of a dramatic change in the course of the Bow River brought about by glaciation. At one time the river flowed north of Tunnel Mountain and out of the mountains via the valley holding Lake Minnewanka. As the glaciers retreated at the end of the last ice age, they left terminal moraines, forming natural dams and changing the course of the river. Eventually the backed-up water found an outlet here between Tunnel Mountain and the northwest ridge of Mount Rundle.

Bow Falls

Banff Historic Walk

Exploring Banff's history

Length: 3.3 km (2 mi) roundtrip
Elevation gain: none
Walking time: 1 hr roundtrip
Starting point: Whyte Museum, 111 Bear St., Banff

EASY WALK

As this walk reveals, the town of Banff has been a bustling tourist town for well over a century. While the suggested route can be walked in an hour, plan on a more leisurely pace, with time to read the plaques set in front of each property and to soak up the atmosphere of town.

The starting point of this walk is the **Whyte Museum of the Canadian Rockies** (111 Bear St.), which offers guided walking tours of the town (see *Information* under *Sources*). Beside the museum is the 1907 **Moore Residence** (125 Lynx St.), a distinctive log home with blue shutters that was the first in Banff to have central heating and indoor plumbing. Backing onto the Moore Residence is the **Whyte Residence** (130 Bow Ave.), the 1931 home of prominent Banff residents who were instrumental in preserving the region's history through their establishment of the Whyte Museum. Between

Moore Residence

this home and the museum is a group of simple log cabins, each with a plaque detailing their history.

Walking down Bear Street from the Whyte Museum, the **Old Crag Cabin** (211 Bear St.), dating to the late 1890s, has been incorporated into a

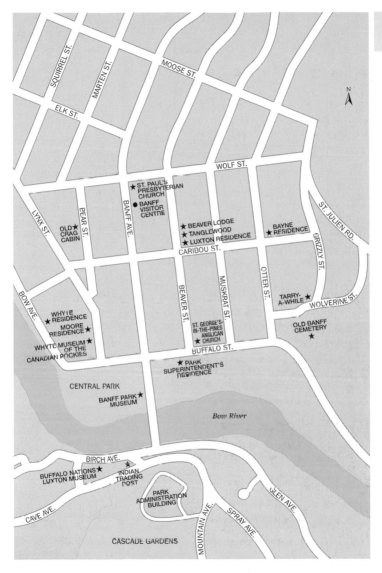

N

★ ST. PAUL'S
PRESBYTERIAN
CHURCH
● BANFF
VISITOR
CENTRE

★ BEAVER LODGE
★ TANGLEWOOD
★ LUXTON RESIDENCE

OLD ★
CRAG
CABIN

BAYNE ★
RESIDENCE

SQUIRREL ST.
MARTEN ST.
MOOSE ST.
ELK ST.
WOLF ST.
LYNX ST.
PEAR ST.
BANFF AVE.
CARIBOU ST.
ST. JULIEN RD.
GRIZZLY ST.

TARRY- ★
A-WHILE

WOLVERINE ST.

OTTER ST.

OLD BANFF
CEMETERY
★

WHYLE ★
RESIDENCE
MOORE
RESIDENCE ★

WHYTE MUSEUM
OF THE
CANADIAN ROCKIES

BOW AVE.

BEAVER ST.

MUSKRAT ST.

ST. GEORGE'S-
IN-THE-PINES
ANGLICAN
CHURCH

BUFFALO ST.

★ PARK
SUPERINTENDENT'S
RESIDENCE

CENTRAL PARK

BANFF PARK ★
MUSEUM

Bow River

BIRCH AVE.

BUFFALO NATIONS ★
LUXTON MUSEUM

INDIAN
TRADING
POST

PARK
ADMINISTRATION
BUILDING

CAVE AVE.

MOUNTAIN AVE.

SPRAY AVE.

GLEN AVE.

CASCADE GARDENS

The middle building in this 1888 painting is thought to depict Tanglewood.

modern shopping plaza. Continue north along Bear Street, and turn right onto Wolf Street. Across Banff Avenue is **St. Paul's Presbyterian Church** (230 Banff Ave.), a Gothic Revival building dating to 1930 (note the shape of Mount Rundle in the stained glass window above the front entrance). Continuing toward Tunnel Mountain on Wolf Street, turn right down Beaver Street, where a row of historic properties has been preserved. The oldest of these is **Tanglewood** (208 Beaver St.), thought to have originally been built as a post office in 1887. Beside Tanglewood is the **Luxton Residence,** which

The Luxton Residence dates to 1905.

was home to the prominent Luxton family for 90 years. On the other side of Tanglewood is **Beaver Lodge,** an eight-room log boarding house that has changed little in appearance since 1913.

One block back from Beaver Street, at the corner of Caribou and Otter Streets, is the **Bayne Residence** (202 Otter St.). With an elaborate porch and distinctive brickwork, and cobblestone foundations, it presents itself as the home of an upper class Banff family from a century ago. Continue uphill and turn right along Grizzly Street to reach **Tarry-A-**

While (117 Grizzly St.), the 1911 home of Mary Schäffer, one of the Canadian Rockies' most energetic female pioneers. Across the road is **Old Banff Cemetery**, the resting place of many Banff pioneers. Walking back toward Banff Avenue, **St. George's-in-the-Pines Anglican Church** was completed in 1926 and across Buffalo Street is the **Park Superintendent's Residence**. This grand log building was built in 1920 and still serves as the home of the park's superintendent.

St. George's-in-the-Pines Anglican Church

Crossing the Bow River Bridge, the **Park Administration Building** looms ahead. This 1935 Tudor Revival-style building is surrounded by the colourful flowerbeds and stone walkways of **Cascade Gardens**. Across Cave Avenue is the **Indian Trading Post**, Banff's oldest gift store. It opened in 1904 selling beadwork and furs traded from the Stoney people and still specializes in native arts and crafts. Behind the gift shop is the **Buffalo Nations Luxton Museum** (Birch St.), a log stockade dedicated to telling the story of the First Nations people.

From this museum, head back across the river to the **Banff Park Museum**. Built in 1903, its displays of stuffed animals are a classic example of changing park values since an era when visitors would "experience" the park by viewing this museum's exhibits and its adjacent zoo (which has long since disappeared).

Cascade Gardens

Fenland

Nature on the back doorstep

Length: 2.1 km (1.3 mi) roundtrip
Elevation gain: none
Walking time: 30 minutes roundtrip
Starting point: Forty Mile Picnic Area, Mt. Norquay Rd., across the railway tracks from downtown Banff
Origin of the name: An old English word used to describe marshland

EASY WALK

This short but interesting walk on the edge of town loops through forest at the eastern edge of the Vermilion Lakes marshland. The trail runs beside the meandering waters of Echo and Forty Mile

Forty Mile Creek

Creeks and loops through a spruce forest carpeted with bunchberry and a green cloud of horsetails.

From Forty Mile Picnic Area, cross a bridge over the creek and continue to a trail split.

Take the left fork and walk the loop in a clockwise direction for trail markers to correspond with the order presented on a brochure available at the trailhead. Trail highlights include bear claw marks on aspen, an old beaver lodge and canals, and the

Elk are common along the Fenland trail.

Fenland's role as an elk nursery (the trail is closed during spring calving season).

Options: Due to its proximity to downtown Banff, many people reach Fenland by walking along the Bow River from Central Park, past the canoe dock, and then following a paved road closed to traffic to Railway Avenue. Cross the tracks and look for the trail to the left, which links onto Fenland.

Another option is to extend your walk beyond Fenland to **Vermilion Lakes Drive**. Popular with walkers and cyclists, this road passes three shallow lakes and postcard views of Mount Rundle over a span of 4.5 kilometres (2.8 miles). Access to the road is from the north end of the Fenland loop.

This trail is named for its marshy environment.

Marsh Loop

Marching around a marsh

Length: 2.3 km (1.4 mi) roundtrip
Elevation gain: minimal
Walking time: 40 minutes roundtrip
Starting point: Cave and Basin National Historic Site,
1.6 km (1 mi) along Cave Ave. from the Bow River Bridge
Origin of the name: A wetland filled by water from hot springs

EASY WALK

No visit to the Cave and Basin is complete without visiting the marsh below the historic hot springs complex. Most visitors get as far as the boardwalks and their interpretive displays, but you can continue beyond to make a full circuit of this remarkable wetland.

From the large parking lot, walk uphill to the Cave and Basin National Historic Site, where the Marsh Trail, a boardwalk, leads down to a bird-blind overlooking the wetlands. Back at the top of this interpretive trail, follow the paved pathway alongside the Cave and Basin complex to a trailhead kiosk just beyond the rise. From this point, it's 700 metres (0.4 miles) downhill along a paved pathway to the Bow River. Sundance Canyon (see

early morning along Marsh Loop

page 40) lies ahead, while the Marsh Loop cuts back to the right onto a wide but rough trail. It runs downstream along the banks of the river, with the marsh coming into view on the right after a few minutes' walking. After one

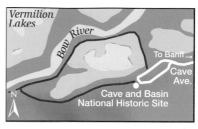

kilometre (0.6 miles), the trail turns sharply to the right and follows an earthen dike back to the parking lot.

The marsh is unique in that it is fed by hotsprings flowing out of the lower slopes of Sulphur Mountain through faults in the bedrock. The water has cooled considerably by the time it flows into these wetlands, but it remains warm enough that the wetlands closest to the mountain remain ice-free in winter. This creates a habitat for exotic plant life such as orchids, stickleback fish, and otherwise migratory birds that remain year-round.

looking across the Bow River from along Marsh Loop

Cascade Ponds

Pathways and a picnic

Length: 1.2 km (0.7 mi) roundtrip
Elevation gain: none
Walking time: 15 minutes
Starting point: Lake Minnewanka Rd., 300 m (0.2 mi) north of
Trans-Canada Hwy.
Origin of the name: A cascading waterfall (see *Options,* below)

EASY WALK

Cascade Mountain and its namesake waterfall is your constant companion on this short stroll around linked ponds.

Cascade Ponds was created when gravel pits were transformed to a day use area, complete with wooden bridges, grassy banks, picnic tables, firepits, and cooking shelters. It's a popular spot for dog

Cascade Ponds is a beautiful spot for a stroll.

walkers and picnicking, while the brave swim in the cold water. The entire area is encircled by a walking trail, with a shortcut over two bridges dividing the lake into two "ponds." Heading off in a counter-clockwise direction from the parking lot, the pathway follows the ponds to their outlet, where water flows over a concrete wall into a shallow pool. Across the barrier and looping around the lake's deepest point, Cascade Mountain, with its distinctive waterfall, rises majestically across the water. From this point, it's easy to see why the natives knew the mountain as *minihapa,* which translates to "mountain where the water falls." Continuing around the ponds, distinctive Mt. Alymer can be seen to the north.

Options: The cascade from which the ponds take their name can be reached along the **Cascade Falls Trail**. This short walk begins across Lake Minnewanka Rd. from the Cascade Ponds access road. After skirting the end of an airfield, this rocky trail climbs through a forest of aspen poplar. Around 600 metres (0.4 miles) from the road, it emerges beside a creek bed. Above this point, the lower of two ledges is wide and offers valley views. The panorama is better from above, where the sweeping panorama includes Cascade Ponds, Mount Rundle, and mountain peaks beyond Canmore. In winter, this is one of the park's most popular ice-climbing spots.

Cascade Falls

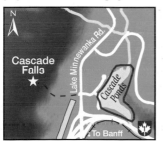

Bankhead Interpretive Walk

Explore the park's coal-mining past

Length: 1 km (0.6 miles) roundtrip
Elevation loss: minimal
Walking time: 15 minutes roundtrip
Starting point: Lake Minnewanka Rd., 3 km (1.9 mi) from the Trans-Canada Hwy.
Origin of the name: A Scottish town

EASY WALK

The arrival of the railway in 1883 spurred development of coal deposits near the base of Cascade Mountain and by 1904 a large mining operation was in full swing. Following a 1922 miners' strike, the mine closed and the town's residents moved on. Today, you can walk an interpretive trail that loops through the remains of the industrial operation on the valley floor.

The tipple, where coal was sorted, was the largest building at Bankhead.

A lookout at the parking lot allows for an overview of the area, while interpretive boards along a short loop trail down on the valley floor describe the large-

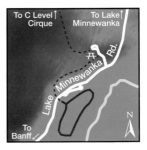

scale sorting and processing plant through which up to 500,000 tons of coal passed annually. When the mine closed, most of the buildings were demolished, leaving concrete foundations that are slowly being reclaimed by Mother Nature. The old transformer building is an exception, and visitors can peer through its windows to view displays relating to the mine's past. You will also pass by vintage coal cars on a short stretch of narrow-gauge railway, showing how coal was moved from the mine to the valley floor.

Bankhead foundations are slowly being overgrown by vegetation.

Options: An unmarked trail opposite the parking lot climbs to Upper Bankhead Picnic Area. This was originally the site of the town of Bankhead, with a bustling main street and almost 1,000 residents. Returning to the Bankhead Interpretive Walk via the road, the front steps of a once-grand church are passed on the left. You can also visit remnants of the coal operation along the hiking trail to **C Level Cirque** (see page 50).

These rail cars were originally used to haul coal from the mine to the valley floor.

Lake Minnewanka

A lakeside stroll to a water-filled canyon

Length: 1.5 km (0.9 miles) to Stewart Canyon
Elevation gain: minimal
Walking time: 20 minutes one way
Starting point: Lake Minnewanka day use area, 5.5 km (3.5 mi) along Lake Minnewanka Rd. from the Trans-Canada Hwy.
Origin of the name: A native word that translates to "lake of the water spirit"

EASY WALK

The majority of visitors only walk along the shoreline of the park's largest lake for 20 minutes or so, as far as **Stewart Canyon**, but it's possible to continue further—much further—and make a full day of it. Due to its low elevation and location in the Front Ranges, this is an attractive area to explore early and late in the hiking season.

The trail hugs the shore of Lake Minnewanka.

The southwest end of Lake Minnewanka is a busy place. A marina is home to a tour boat operation, anglers head out in their boats chasing lake trout, scuba divers descend to the remnants of a submerged town, and picnickers flock to tables spread along the lakeshore. Follow the paved path along the lake beyond these crowds to where a narrow trail dives headlong into a forest of lodgepole pine. Views along this section of trail extend across the water to the steep slopes of Mt. Inglismaldie while below are pebbly beaches strewn with driftwood. Straight ahead is the Palliser Range, where the effects of fire can clearly be seen on the lower slopes. Long and narrow Stewart Canyon, spanned by a high footbridge, is soon reached. Created by a fault in the bedrock, it is where the Cascade River flows into Lake Minnewanka, but when the water level is high it becomes an arm of the lake.

Stewart Canyon

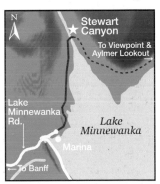

Options: Beyond the Stewart Canyon bridge, the trail becomes narrower as it climbs over a low, forested ridge, then rolls along the north shore for 20 kilometres (12 miles). Campsites and the Aylmer Lookout trail are destinations for backpackers along this lengthy shoreline trail. However, casual hikers often turn around 1.5 kilometres (0.9 miles) beyond the canyon, where there's an elevated viewpoint overlooking the lake.

Johnson Lake

Summer recreation hotspot

Length: 3.5 km (2.2 mi) roundtrip
Elevation gain: minimal
Walking time: 1 hour roundtrip
Starting point: 2.2 km (1.4 mi) off the Lake Minnewanka Rd., 4.6 km (2.9 mi) from the Trans-Canada Hwy.
Origin of the name: Unknown

EASY WALK

Throughout the warmest weeks of summer, the beach at the west end of Johnson Lake is a playground for Banff residents. But this small lake has much to offer beyond swimming and sunbathing, as the trail around its shoreline reveals a perfect example of low-elevation montane forest. Often snowfree by late April, expect to observe nesting waterfowl in the spring and muskrat in the marshy areas.

The beach at Johnson Lake gets very busy.

From the parking lot, walk downhill and across a small earth-fill dam and bridge. Beyond the bridge, the trail angles uphill briefly beneath a powerline, then branches left into the forest where it rolls along through a dense forest of pine and spruce above the lake's south shore. In May, the forest floor is alive with the blooms of purple calypso orchids.

At the far end of the lake, the trail crosses an earthen dike, where you get your first good views down the length of this peaceful lake to Cascade Mountain. Returning along the north

the view across Johnson Lake to Mt. Rundle

shore, there are grassy slopes and an open forest of Douglas fir and low growing junipers. The trail reaches the trailhead and beach after a short detour around a marshy bay created by a small tributary stream (watch for waterfowl and muskrat).

Muskrats are common near the end of the loop.

Tunnel Mountain

Summit a mountain before breakfast

Length: 2.3 km (1.4 mi) one way
Elevation gain: 240 m (790 ft)
Walking time: 40 minutes one way
Starting point: Banff Centre overflow parking lot, along St. Julien Rd. uphill from Wolf St.
Origin of the name: An early plan had the Canadian Pacific Railway blasting a tunnel through this mountain

SHORT HIKE

The trail to the summit of Tunnel Mountain is one of the park's oldest—a popular outing for Banff residents and visitors for over a century. The low summit, 300 metres (980 feet) above the town, offers wonderful views of the Banff environs, including the Banff Springs Hotel and a section of the Bow Valley. The trail's broad track

and well-graded switchbacks are worthy of royalty (it was rebuilt in 1939 so King George VI could climb the mountain during his cross-Canada tour with Queen Elizabeth).

The first 400 metres (0.2 miles) of trail climbs through forest from St. Julien Road to Tunnel Mountain Road, where a small parking area serves as an alternate trailhead (drive here if you want to shorten the hike). After crossing Tunnel Mountain Road, the trail switchbacks upwards through dense stands of lodgepole pine and Douglas fir with occasional

The Banff Springs Golf Course is laid out below Tunnel Mountain.

the town of Banff from Tunnel Mountain

openings overlooking the town and valley. When you reach the summit ridge, 1.9 kilometres (1.2 miles) from the trailhead, views extend across the Bow River to the Banff Springs Hotel. At this point, the trail turns north to skirt along the edge of a sheer cliff (fenced for your safety), and views open eastward to the Banff Springs Golf Course and across the Bow River to the massive cliffs of Mount Rundle. One last,

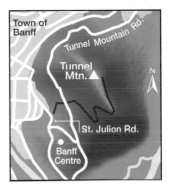

short climb brings you to the sparsely forested 1,690-metre (5,540-foot) summit, where a fire tower once stood. Limestone outcrops just west of the summit overlook the town of Banff, with views extending to Vermilion Lakes and up the Bow Valley to the Massive Range. This is a good place to appreciate the mountain's geological history—while surrounding mountains such as Rundle and Cascade escaped the effects of glaciation during the last ice age, the lower summit of Tunnel Mountain was smoothed by glaciers.

Hoodoos

Distinctive geological formations

Length: 5.1 km (3.2 mi) one way
Elevation gain: 60 m (200 ft)
Walking time: 1.5 hours one way
Starting point: Surprise Corner. Follow Buffalo St. southeast from
Banff Ave. for 1.2 km (0.7 mi)
Origin of the name: A geological feature found at trail's end

SHORT HIKE

You can reach the hoodoos on a paved nature trail running from Tunnel Mountain Road, or take a more interesting approach to these intriguing geological formations by hiking beneath Tunnel Mountain from Surprise Corner. The route is particularly rewarding in June and July, when meadows are filled with the blooms of blue flax, harebells, and gaillardia.

From Surprise Corner viewpoint, the trail descends to the Bow River and then follows beneath the towering cliffs that form Tunnel Mountain's east face. At km 1.6 (mile 1.0), the river splits and the trail follows the bank of the west channel through an open forest where elk often graze. Soon you are climbing through open stands of aspen, lodgepole pine and Douglas fir to Tunnel Mountain Road. From this point, the trail parallels the road the rest of the way to the hoodoos parking area. A variety of viewpoints with interpretive

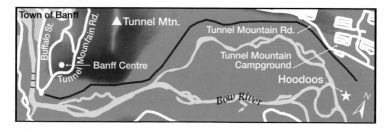

displays are spread along the final 500-metre-long (0.3-mile) stretch of trail.

The hoodoos are weirdly shaped pillars rising from a steep ridge overlooking the Bow River. They are carved from the glacial till that composes the ridge. As the ridge eroded, some of the rock, gravel and sand was cemented by the soil's high lime content and become resistant to weathering. The result is consolidated material standing in the form of pillars.

While you can complete a circuit of Tunnel Mountain by walking back to town along the road, you can also catch a Banff Transit bus that services the nearby campgrounds throughout the summer.

It is impossible not to be intrigued by the weirdly shaped hoodoos at the end of this trail.

The Bow River is rarely out of sight along the Hoodoos Trail.

Sundance Canyon

A riverside stroll to a striking canyon

Length: 5 km (3.1 mi) one way
Elevation gain: 145 m (470 ft)
Walking time: 1.5 hours one way
Starting point: Cave and Basin National Historic Site,
1.6 km (1 mi) along Cave Ave. from the Bow River Bridge
Origin of the name: A ceremonial dance performed by local Stoney
people

SHORT HIKE

Throughout most of its long history, the 2.4-kilometre (1.5-mile) loop trail leading through Sundance Canyon was accessible by road from the town of Banff. In the mid-1980s, the road beyond the Cave and Basin was converted to a paved walking and cycling path,

looking down Sundance Canyon

which made the trip longer but more scenically varied. Today, many people bike to the canyon on the paved trail, but much of the approach follows beside the Bow River and is a pleasant route for walkers as well.

From the Cave and Basin, the paved trail descends gradually through forest to the Bow River. For the next 1.6 kilometres (one mile) it follows along the river and its side channels with views of the rugged peaks to the north, including the distinctive spire of Mount Edith. The final stretch to the canyon climbs

a side channel of the Bow River and the mountains beyond

gradually through forest, passing washrooms and a picnic area at km 3.1 km (mi 1.9), just before pavement and bike access end (bike stands are supplied for cyclists). From this point, the trail climbs steeply into a rugged little canyon, which has been carved into the bedrock of a hanging valley by flowing water. Beyond the top of the canyon, the trail loops back through forest, passing two viewpoints before descending back to the end of the pavement.

Options. On your return from Sundance Canyon, watch for a broad, dirt track that continues along the Bow River where the pavement begins its final climb back to the Cave and Basin. By staying on this trail, you can return to the parking area on the **Marsh Loop** (page 26).

[1] signposted as Cave and Basin National Historic Site

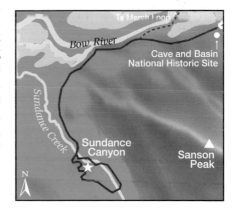

Stoney Squaw

Up close and personal with Cascade Mountain

Length: 2.1 km (1.3 mi) one way
Elevation gain: 238 m (780 ft)
Walking time: 50 minutes one way
Starting point: Ski Norquay, 6 km (3.7 mi) up Mt. Norquay Rd. from the Trans-Canada Hwy.
Origin of the name: the wife of a Stoney warrior who tended to her husband as he lay wounded at the mountain's base

SHORT HIKE

Stoney Squaw is a 1,884-metre-high (6,180-foot) promontory extending east from Mount Norquay. It is one of the highest and

Lichens cover many of the trees in the damp forest.

easily reached viewpoints in the vicinity of the town, and although there are a lot of trees on the summit, a few openings reveal the Bow Valley below.

From a trailhead kiosk to the right as you enter the Ski Norquay parking lot, this moderately graded but steady uphill trail is enclosed in a dense forest of lodgepole pine and spruce most of the way to the summit. It is a relatively damp place, and many of the trees are covered with wispy *bryoria* hair lichen. Upon reaching a ridge at km 1.3 (mi 0.8), head

Cascade Mountain dominates the panorama from Stoney Squaw

left and downhill (the right fork along the ridge leads nowhere). Once near the summit you begin to catch glimpses of the town of Banff and its environs. Tunnel Mountain, Mount Rundle, and Sulphur Mountain are all visible beyond. A little further along, the trail crests the mountain's sheer

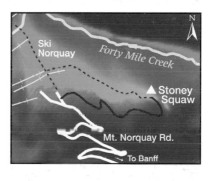

northeastern face, where views extend north across Forty Mile Creek to nearby Cascade Mountain and beyond Cascade Ponds to Mounts Ingismaldie and Girouard.

Options: Most hikers descend the way they came, but it is also possible to continue from the summit to the left, along a trail that follows the cliff line, eventually emerging at a green-roofed building at the ski area. From this point it's a short walk back to the trailhead kiosk through the parking lot.

Sulphur Mountain

An unrelenting climb

Length: 5.5 km (3.4 mi) one way
Elevation gain: 700 m (2,300 ft)
Walking time: 2 to 3 hours one way
Starting point: Upper Hot Springs parking lot, 3.5 km (2.2 mi) from downtown Banff along Mountain Ave.
Origin of the name: Sulphur hot springs at the base of the mountain

DAY TRIP

Tens of thousands of people ride the gondola to the 2,281-metre-high (7,486-foot) summit of Sulphur Mountain each summer to enjoy one of the most famous views in Canada—a 360-degree panorama encompassing the town of Banff, the Banff Springs Hotel, and surrounding mountains. It is also possible to walk up the mountain, with the option of purchasing a one-way gondola ticket and returning to the valley floor in just eight minutes.

The trail switchbacks under the Banff Gondola multiple times.

While the trail gains 700 metres (2,300 feet) of elevation, 28 switchbacks keep the grade reasonable. The track is wide as it climbs from the Upper Hot Springs parking lot and begins a somewhat-tedious ascent of the mountain. Though the climb is forested throughout, views over the town and valley do open briefly as you pass just north of a waterfall on the mountain's east slope. The grade steepens as the trail nears the summit and begins switchbacking beneath the gondola line. A few scattered alpine larch in the dense forest herald the summit ridge and the upper gondola terminal with its restaurants and much-needed refreshment kiosk.

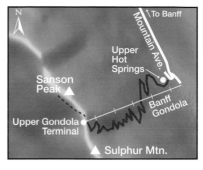

Options: For most visitors, this will be one of the most appealing options detailed in this guidebook—the **Banff Gondola** (403/762-2523, www.banffgondola.com) whisks visitors to the summit of Sulphur Mountain, from where you can admire the view, stroll along the boardwalk, and enjoy a meal at one of three eateries.

From the upper gondola terminal, you can follow a boardwalk leading 600 metres (0.4 miles) to the summit of **Sanson Peak**, where there is a stone weather observatory built in 1903. The peak is named for park meteorologist Norman Sanson, who hiked up the mountain over 1,000 times to take readings at this observatory.

A boardwalk leads to Sanson Peak.

Spray River

A pleasant but unremarkable trek into the wilderness surrounding town

Length: 6.5 km (4 mi) one way
Elevation gain: 75 m (250 ft)
Walking time: 2 hrs one way
Starting point: Beyond Bow Falls, park just over the Spray River Bridge. Walk along Golf Course Rd. 300 m (0.2 mi) to the trailhead on the right-hand side of the road.
Origin of the name: A descriptive name from spray given off by nearby Bow Falls

DAY TRIP

This lengthy but easy loop runs up one side of the Spray River and back down the other. It follows abandoned fire roads most of the way, there is little gain or loss of elevation, making it a pleasant, undemanding outing for hikers as well as a favourite trip for mountain bikers and cross-country skiers.

Follow the broad, dirt track skirting through the forest behind the green and fairway to a signed junction. From this point you can hike

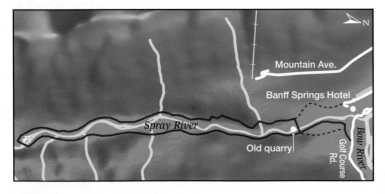

the circuit clockwise by turning left or, our preference, counter-clockwise by keeping right. Either way, you will return to this junction at the completion of the circuit. By staying right, you climb over a forested rise to the Spray River. Follow the river upstream for one kilometre (0.6 miles) to a footbridge, which is beside an old limestone quarry. Rundle rock used to construct the Banff Springs Hotel was excavated from this site, and from the bridge, views extend back to the hotel. (The trail to this point and then back to the hotel is known locally as Old Quarry Loop.) Across the river, follow the trail up through the forest and turn up-valley (left) onto abandoned fire road. It's five kilometres (3.1 miles) from this point to a junction and picnic area on open flats beside the river. From this point, turn left and cross the footbridge to return down the east side of the river. Scenery is a bit more pleasant and varied along this section of the trail, rolling through forest and climbing gradually to an open benchland overlooking the river and the Banff Springs Hotel, which rises from the forest like a medieval castle. From this viewpoint, a short, gradual descent brings you back to the initial trail junction and Golf Course Road.

one of two foot bridges across the Spray River

Aspen poplar brighten a fall walk along the Spray River.

Rundle Riverside

Linking Banff and Canmore

Length: 14.6 km (9.1 mi) one way
Elevation gain: 135 m (450 ft)
Walking time: 4 to 5 hours one way
Starting point: Golf Course Rd., 4.1 km (2.5 mi) from Bow Falls
(take the right fork after 2.7 km/1.7 mi)
Origin of the name: Reverend Robert Terrill Rundle, the valley's
first missionary

DAY TRIP

M ore popular with mountain bikers than hikers, Rundle Riverside
links Banff with the nearby town of Canmore. Along the way,
there are numerous opportunities to stop and relax beside the river,
and the sheer buttresses of Mount Rundle, visible through the trees,

a quiet stretch of water along Rundle Riverside

are constant companions. The trail is rough, forest-enclosed, and sometimes very rocky (it crosses three major outwashes), so hikers will definitely find the trip more relaxing than those on bikes.

The trail reaches the Bow River 400 metres (0.2 miles) beyond the trailhead kiosk—a peaceful spot with a nice view of the distant Fairholme Range—then stays close to its true right bank for the next four kilometres (2.5 miles). The last access to the river is at km 4.9 (mi 3), where the trail angles off to the right and starts climbing to the boundary of Banff National Park at km 8.4 (mi 5.2). Once beyond the park, the trail becomes a wide gravel track rising steeply into the midst of the Canmore Nordic Centre, where the cross-country skiing and biathlon events of the 1988 Winter Olympic Games were staged. This smooth roadbed leads you through the maze of trails (follow signs indicating "Back to Day Lodge" at

You share the final section of the Rundle Riverside Trail with world-class athletes.

trail intersections). The trail's highest elevation, 180 metres (590 feet) above the Bow River, is reached in the middle of a large, grassy clearing (the remnants of strip mining). One last descent brings you to the Canmore Nordic Centre day lodge, which is four kilometres (2.5 miles) from downtown Canmore via the Spray Lakes Road.

Some cyclists return to Banff on the Trans-Canada Highway. One-way hikers and cyclists will need to arrange transportation between the two trailheads.

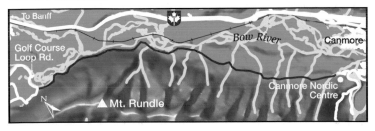

C Level Cirque

Human history and summer snow

Length: 3.9 km (2.4 mi) one way
Elevation gain: 455 m (1,500 ft)
Walking time: 1.5 hours one way
Starting point: Upper Bankhead Picnic Area, 3.5 km (2 mi) along
Lake Minnewanka Rd. from the Trans-Canada Hwy.
Origin of the name: A coalmine and the French word for a bowl-shaped
valley eroded by glacial action

DAY TRIP

This moderately steep trail climbs along the eastern slope of Cascade Mountain to a lofty rockbound sanctuary inhabited by hoary marmots, pikas and, in springtime, wood ticks (beware the latter). Along the way you pass artifacts from the park's coal mining past and an outstanding viewpoint for Lake Minnewanka.

The trail begins its ascent through a pleasantly varied forest of lodgepole pine, aspen, and spruce, where calypso orchids, blue clematis, and many colourful violets bloom in early summer. Within

Lake Minnewanka from the C Level Cirque Trail

20 minutes, the concrete shell of a building associated with the C Level of the Bankhead coal mine (see page 30) is reached. Beyond the crumbling ruin, a faint side trail leads to a ridge of coal tailings providing an excellent view out to Lake Minnewanka. The Palliser Range stretches away from the

northern shoreline, while Mount Inglismaldie and the Fairholme Range rise above the lake to the east. Back on the main trail, you pass several fenced holes, which were air vents for the mineshafts below. The rest of the hike is a steady climb through forest until, just before reaching the cirque, views open down the Bow Valley.

Though the glacier that produced C Level Cirque has long since disappeared, snow often lingers in the basin into midsummer. As the snowbank retreats, a carpet of yellow glacier lilies spreads across the damp, subalpine soil. From the rockslide at the edge of the cirque, a trail continues up to the right along a sparsely forested ridge to an even higher vantage point. However, most hikers prefer to "boot ski" the snowfield beneath Cascade's cliffs or simply relax on a convenient rock to watch the antics of the local inhabitants—marmots, pikas, and golden-mantled ground squirrels.

C Level Cirque

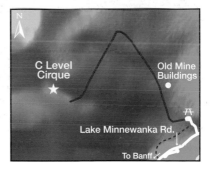

Cascade Amphitheatre

Flower-filled meadows surrounded by towering rock walls

Length: 6.6 km (4.1 mi) one way
Elevation gain: 640 m (2,100 ft)
Walking time: 3 hrs one way
Starting point: Ski Norquay, 6 km (3.7 mi) up Mt. Norquay Rd. from the Trans-Canada Hwy.
Origin of the name: A cascading waterfall on the mountain's east slope

DAY TRIP

The full-day trek to Cascade Amphitheatre and back is not for the faint of heart. After an initial loss of elevation, the trail climbs steadily up Cascade Mountain's west slope, then enters a hanging valley enclosed by limestone cliffs and filled with lush wildflower meadows and rockslides inhabited by marmots and pikas.

Mt. Louis is easily recognized.

The trailhead kiosk is on the right at the beginning of the ski area parking lot (this is the trailhead for Stoney Squaw, see page 42), but to access the trail to Cascade Amphitheatre, walk past the day lodge (closed in summer) on a service road. Just before the Spirit Chairlift, the signed trail ducks off to the right then emerges at the Mystic Chairlift. Beyond this chairlift, follow the trail down through the forest to a junction with the Forty Mile

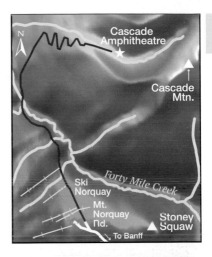

Creek trail at km 2.9 (mi 1.8). Take the right fork to reach the bridged creek. Beyond this point, the trail climbs and the forest opens to a view of the sheer face of Mount Louis. The last trail fork is 1.2 kilometres (0.7 miles) beyond the Forty Mile Creek bridge, where the Amphitheatre trail branches uphill to the right from the Elk Summit trail. A relentless series

Pikas make their home in rocky areas of Cascade Amphitheatre.

of switchbacks transport you upwards through a dense forest of spruce and lodgepole pine for 2.3 kilometres (1.4 miles) to the cool, subalpine forest at the mouth of the amphitheatre.

From the amphitheatre entrance, 6.6 kilometres (4.1 miles) from the trailhead, it's one kilometre (0.6 miles) to a headwall below Cascade Mountain's summit ridge. The moist meadows along the way are carpeted with wildflowers throughout much of the summer, beginning with white-flowered western anemone and yellow glacier lilies along the edges of receding snow banks in late June.

It takes less than one hour to drive between the town of Banff and Lake Louise, but there are many reasons to plan on taking longer. Trails leading off the busy Trans-Canada Highway lead to high alpine lakes, to the colourful wildflowers of Sunshine Meadows, and to a remote backcountry lodge. Along the quieter Bow Valley Parkway, Johnston Canyon is the most popular stop, but trails also lead to a lofty alpine pass, mineral springs, and up the slopes of distinctive Castle Mountain.

Rock Isle Lake, Sunshine Meadows

Muleshoe

Uphill all the way

Length: 1 km (0.6 mi) one way
Elevation gain: 255 m (840 ft)
Walking time: 40 minutes one way
Starting point: Muleshoe Picnic Area, 5.5 km (3.4 mi) west along the Bow Valley Parkway from the Trans-Canada Hwy.
Origin of the name: Descriptive name for the shape of a lake in the valley below

SHORT HIKE

One of the steepest short hikes in Banff National Park, the Muleshoe trail rises quickly through burned forest to lush montane meadows and expansive views of the Bow Valley, Castle Mountain, and Mount Temple near Lake Louise.

Fire has affected much of this side of the valley.

Starting from the trail sign opposite Muleshoe Picnic Area, a narrow path climbs through a stand of aspen poplar before entering a fire-blackened

lodgepole pine-Douglas fir forest. This fire was set by park wardens in May 1993 in their on-going efforts to restore the once naturally occurring montane forest fire regime to this section of the valley. After traversing steeply to the right across the slope, the trail turns uphill and becomes extremely steep. You finally struggle out of partially-burned forest and into a meadow, angling left to the edge of a large gully filled with burned trees. The trail levels out briefly here, where you have the best viewpoint for the valley. From the trail summit, Muleshoe Lake is easily distinguished far below. The small, U-shaped lake was once a channel of the Bow River, but was isolated from the main river by railway construction.

Options: A steep but well-defined track continues upwards along the gully and into subalpine forest, climbing another two kilometres (1.2 miles) to a promontory on the west ridge of **Mount Cory.** This extension is not worthwhile since it stays mainly in the forest and views are limited.

Note: While the Muleshoe trail makes an ideal spring hike, you should check yourself for ticks after returning from a springtime hike.

the view from the top

Johnston Canyon

Busy but beautiful

Length: 2.7 km (1.7 mi) one way
Elevation gain: 135 m (440 ft)
Walking time: 50 minutes one way
Starting point: Johnston Canyon Resort, 17.5 km (11 mi) northwest along the Bow Valley Parkway from the Trans-Canada Hwy.
Origin of the name: A prospector who came to the area in the 1880s

SHORT HIKE

Walking to the two main waterfalls of Johnston Canyon has been fashionable since the first road to Lake Louise was completed

Catwalks add to the fun of exploring Johnston Canyon.

in 1921. The canyon's popularity led to the construction of canyon-clinging catwalks and cliff-mounting staircases, which improved safety and enhanced the visitor experience. Today, the trail to Lower and Upper Falls is busier than ever, and you'll have to arrive in the evening or early morning to avoid the crowds.

Beginning from behind the restaurant and gift shop at Johnston Canyon Resort, the trail begins as a wide paved path climbing gently through the forest. It then descends and stays

Lower Falls

close to Johnston Creek all the way to Lower Falls. Along the way you pass over sturdy iron catwalks attached beneath overhanging canyon walls, where the turbulent waters of the creek flow beneath your feet. Lower Falls is reached after 1.1 kilometres (0.7 miles). A bridge across the creek serves as the main viewpoint for the thundering cataract, but a short tunnel through the canyon bedrock allows passage to an even more intimate vantage point (albeit a wet one). Back on the main trail, you continue up the canyon via more catwalks and broad, well-graded trail. There are many viewpoints overlooking the canyon and a small waterfall. Along

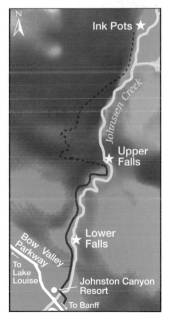

Upper Falls

this section of trail, solitary, slate-grey birds called dippers, or water ouzels, are often seen bouncing up and down on streamside rocks and diving into the rushing water to feed.

At the 30-metre-high (100-foot) **Upper Falls**, there are two viewpoints: the bottom of the falls is reached by a metal catwalk leading to a viewing platform while a short, steep climb on the main trail takes you to a cantilevered platform overlooking the top of the falls. Rock slabs near the brink of the falls are fenced, but some people still clamber through to be near the creek. Always take care on this trail, especially with children, and never cross fences for a closer view.

Options: Only a small percentage of those who reach the Upper Falls continue a further three kilometres (1.9 miles) to the **Ink Pots.** Above Upper Falls, this trail climbs out of the canyon and at the two-kilometre (1.2-mile) mark crests a ridge before descending to open meadows and the seven cold mineral springs. While the springs are unique (they have a constant temperature of 4°C/39°F and their basins are composed of quicksand), many hikers find the extended journey above the canyon a bit of a disappointment. Hopefully open views of the Johnston Creek Valley from the log benches set around the ponds offer some consolation. Allow one hour to reach the Ink Pots from the Upper Falls.

Water bubbling up from deep below the Earth's surface leaves distinctive rings in the Ink Pots.

The Ink Pots lie in a remote meadow beyond the canyon.

Castle Lookout

Sweeping valley views in the shadow of a castle

Length: 3.8 km (2.4 mi) one way
Elevation gain: 550 m (1,800 ft)
Walking time: 1.5 to 2 hours one way
Starting point: Bow Valley Parkway, 5 km (3 mi) west from Castle Junction
Origin of the name: A descriptive name given to Castle Mountain for its fortress-like appearance

SHORT HIKE

This steep trail leads to the site of an old fire lookout on the mid-slopes of Castle Mountain. From this open ridge. there is a panorama of the Bow Valley from the limestone peaks near the town of Banff to the glaciated summits above Lake Louise. Since the trail ascends a southwest-facing slope, it is one of the earliest trails at this elevation to be free of snow in the spring (early to mid-May) and one of the last to remain snowfree in fall.

Spruce grouse are common along lower elevations of this trail.

From the parking area, follow a steep, wide pathway upward through a forest of lodgepole pine, spruce, and occasional Douglas fir. The dense forest allows only a few glimpses of the Bow Valley over the first two kilometres (1.2 miles), but a collapsed log cabin dating to a short-lived mining boom offers a stop of interest after 1.4 kilometres (0.9 miles). The broad trail eventually reverts to single-track and traverses onto steep, sparsely forested slopes overlooking the Bow Valley.

Hikers reaching Castle Lookout are rewarded with sweeping valley views.

In early summer this open forest produces a colourful array of wildflowers, including Indian paintbrush, columbine, and heart-leaved arnica. As you gain elevation, views up and down the Bow Valley improve. Finally the trail twists up through a cliff band, enters a stand of

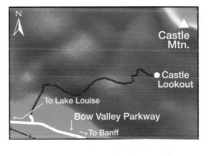

whitebark pine, and contours to the right above the precipice for 100 metres (330 feet) to the foundations of the lookout, which was abandoned by Parks Canada in the mid-1970s.

Note: While the Castle Lookout trail makes an ideal spring hike, you should check yourself for ticks after returning from springtime hike.

Boom Lake

A simple walk to a backcountry lake

Length: 5.1 km (3.2 mi) one way
Elevation gain: 175 m (575 ft)
Walking time: 1.5 hours one way
Starting point: Hwy. 93, 7 km (4.3 mi) west of Castle Junction
Origin of the name: A natural log boom where driftwood is intercepted by an ancient moraine

SHORT HIKE

The Boom Lake trail is an easy walk to a beautifully formed lake contained by a massive 600-metre-high (1,800-foot) limestone wall and glacier-mantled peaks. The trail is often snowfree (but still wet) in early June, which makes it a popular early season outing. It is also fun to visit the lake in late spring and early summer when the snowpack on Boom Mountain is breaking up and where, on a sunny day, you can see and hear avalanches roaring down the mountain's north face.

After crossing pretty Boom Creek at the trailhead, the trail begins a steady climb into dense, subalpine forest and stays well north of the

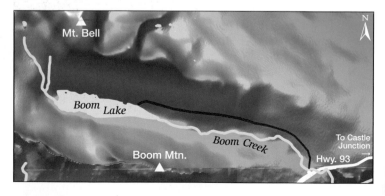

Boom Lake

stream all the way to the lake. The track is wide and the grade is gentle throughout, but streamlets make it a bit sloppy early in the season. However, the runoff redeems itself by creating a well-watered forest with lush undergrowth. Just before reaching the lake, the trail narrows to a traditional footpath and ends abruptly at a rockslide that has tumbled down from the slope to the north into the eastern end of the lake. A bit of rock-hopping will get you to the water's edge. The broad north face of Boom Mountain soars above the lake's south shore, and the glaciated spires of Quadra Mountain (3,173 metres/10,410 feet) and Bident Mountain (3,084 metres/10,120 feet) rise beyond its far end.

This ancient rockslide ends at the lake.

Cory Pass

A test of fitness

Length: 5.8 km (3.6 mi) one way
Elevation gain: 915 m (3,000 ft)
Walking time: 3 hours one way
Starting point: Fireside Picnic Area, signposted 500 m (0.3 mi) along the Bow Valley Parkway from the Trans-Canada Hwy.
Origin of the name: William Wallace Cory, an early government official

DAY TRIP

Cory Pass is the most spectacular hike along the Bow Valley Parkway and one of the most strenuous in park. The 2,300-meter-high (7,500-foot) pass frames the sheer spire of Mount Louis, a view usually reserved for mountaineers—and you will feel like one after ascending nearly one vertical kilometre (3,000 feet) to get there.

From Fireside Picnic Area, the trail runs through coniferous forest and pleasant aspen groves to a junction at km 1.1 (0.7 mi). The trail to Cory Pass cuts uphill to the left at this split and begins a heart-pounding climb on an open, south-facing slope. After a brief respite on a grassy knoll overlooking the Bow Valley, it continues its relentless ascent for another 1.3 kilometres (0.8 miles) to a forested ridge and the first views of your objective—the lofty notch of Cory Pass. You climb along this rocky, sparsely forested ridge for another one kilometre (0.6 miles) to

Before beginning its climb, the trail passes through a forest of aspen poplar.

the top of a small cliff band, which requires that you down-climb through an obvious but steep break in the rock. (Nothing serious, but you will have to use your hands to steady yourself.) The trail picks up again at the base of this cliff and, a few moments later, emerges from the trees and ascends across a long open slope to the pass.

Cory Pass is often a very cold and windy place. Sandwiched between the cliffs of Mounts Edith to the east and Cory to the west, this high, rockbound gap might more appropriately be considered a *col* (a French term for a high gap between two peaks). However, the views are worth any discomforts of trail or pass, highlighted by the towering slabs of grey limestone that form the east face of Mount Louis.

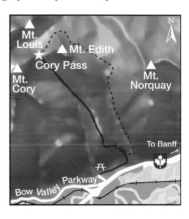

hikers enjoying a well-deserved rest upon reaching Cory Pass

Bourgeau Lake

A demure destination surrounded by striking scenery

Length: 7.5 km (4.6 mi) one way
Elevation gain: 725 m (2,380 ft)
Walking time: 2.5 to 3 hours one way
Starting point: Trans-Canada Hwy., 3 km (1.9 mi) west of the Sunshine Village interchange
Origin of the name: Eugene Bourgeau, a botanist on the 1858 Palliser Expedition

DAY TRIP

Of the numerous high lakes along the Bow Valley, Bourgeau is the nearest to the town of Banff and has been a favoured hiking destination for many decades. Surrounded by lush subalpine meadows and cradled between the highest and most spectacular mountains of the Massive Range, its popularity is well deserved.

The trail climbs through dense forest above the Wolverine Creek Valley and doesn't achieve open views until reaching km 2.4 (mi 1.5), where you can look back over your shoulder to the Bow Valley and the serrated summits of the Sawback Range. After a steady climb

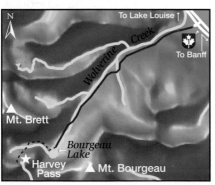

along slopes well above the valley floor, the trail crosses Wolverine Creek beneath a series of waterfalls at km 5.5 (mi 3.4). This is a good spot for a break before tackling the steep switchbacks that complete the climb to the Bourgeau Lake amphitheatre. At the top of this 1.3-kilometre

Bourgeau Lake

(0.8-mile) grade, the trail enters a long meadow—a lush, well-watered area filled with an array of colourful wildflowers through late July and August. At the lake's rocky shore, hikers are welcomed by pikas, golden-mantled ground squirrels, chipmunks, and white-tailed ptarmigan.

Options: Beyond the lake, a steep trail leads to **Harvey Pass**, 2.2 kilometres (1.4 miles) and 310 vertical metres (1,020 feet) from Bourgeau. The signposted trail traverses the forested north shore of Bourgeau Lake, then climbs steeply across an open, rocky slope, where a stream drops from between Mounts Bourgeau and Brett. After skirting a shallow, rockbound lake, it emerges into an alpine bowl, where you turn south (left) and climb to a tiny lake in Harvey Pass. From here, views extend as far as Mount Assiniboine.

This small body of water lies in a wide basin above Bourgeau Lake.

Rockbound Lake

Rugged and remote beauty

Length: 8.4 km (5.2 mi) one way
Elevation gain: 760 m (2,500 ft)
Walking time: 2.5 to 3 hours one way
Starting point: Bow Valley Parkway, just east (toward Banff) from Castle Junction
Origin of the name: A descriptive name for the lake's surroundings

DAY TRIP

Overshadowed by the bastions and turrets of Castle Mountain, Rockbound Lake is a cold, grey body of water contained by steep talus slopes and massive boulder fields. Lush wildflower meadows and tiny Tower Lake on the final approach are an added bonus.

The trail starts on an old access road that climbs gradually through forest along the southern flank of Castle Mountain. Eventually it

It's easy to see how Rockbound Lake got its name.

enters the high valley behind Castle Mountain and, after five kilometres (3.1 miles), narrows to single track. Just a bit farther on, views open to Castle Mountain's Eisenhower Tower, a 2,750-metre-high (9,000-foot) limestone pinnacle rising in front of the main body of the mountain. The trail beyond this point can be rather messy, particularly early in the season when the entire area is soggy from melting snow. An extensive meadow leads to **Tower Lake**, a small body of water set within a semicircle of rock.

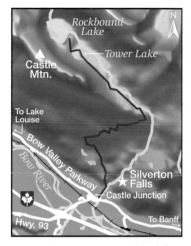

The trail continues to the right of Tower Lake and climbs very steeply up the headwall beyond. Through a scattered forest of Engelmann spruce, alpine fir, and larch at the top of the cliff, you catch your first view of Rockbound Lake and immediately appreciate the aptness of the name. It's tempting to spend an hour or two scrambling among the huge boulders along the lake's southern shore or ascending the slopes of Helena Ridge to the east for a better perspective of the amphitheatre.

Options: Just beyond the trailhead, a short side trail leads to **Silverton Falls**, a staircase-style waterfall hidden in the forest less than one kilometre (0.6 miles) from the trailhead.

Silverton Falls

Sunshine Meadows

The park's most accessible alpine meadows

Access: A shuttle bus operated by **White Mountain Adventures** (403/762-7889 or 800/408-0005; www.sunshinemeadowsbanff.com) departs for Sunshine Meadows mid-June to late Sept. two or three times daily from the parking lot at the base of a gondola leading up to Sunshine Village ski area. To get to the parking lot, take the Trans-Canada Hwy. 9 km (5.6 mi) west from the town of Banff and follow the Sunshine Road for another 9 km (5.6 mi).
Origin of the name: Unknown

DAY TRIP

The Sunshine Meadows region is unique in the Canadian Rockies. Unlike most of the Continental Divide, which is composed of heavily glaciated peaks, this 100-square-kilometre (38-square-mile) stretch is rolling subalpine meadows filled with an incredible variety of wildflowers.

Access to Sunshine Meadows is by shuttle bus.

Although it is possible to reach Sunshine Meadows on foot along a 6.5-kilometre (four-mile) access road (allow two hours one way) from the Sunshine Village parking lot, the vast majority of visitors arrive via the shuttle bus described above. The bus service terminates at the top of the gondola (which only operates in winter), from where the following trails lead through the meadows.

Rock Isle Lake, one of the most photographed scenes in the backcountry of Banff National Park

Rock Isle Lake

Length: 1.8 km (1.1 mi) one way
Elevation gain: 105 m (350 ft)
Walking time: 40 minutes one way

From the shuttle bus drop-off, head uphill on the gravel road and follow the signed trail off to the left. This wide trail ascends to the Continental Divide and crosses into British Columbia's Mount Assiniboine Provincial Park, from where magnificent views stretch across the vast Sunshine Meadows to the distant pyramid of Mount Assiniboine. From here it's a short downhill walk to the viewpoint overlooking Rock Isle Lake. In the early morning, the waters of this small lake are often a mirror reflecting its rocky island and shoreline, and there is a peacefulness and natural symmetry in the scene that has attracted artists and photographers for many decades.

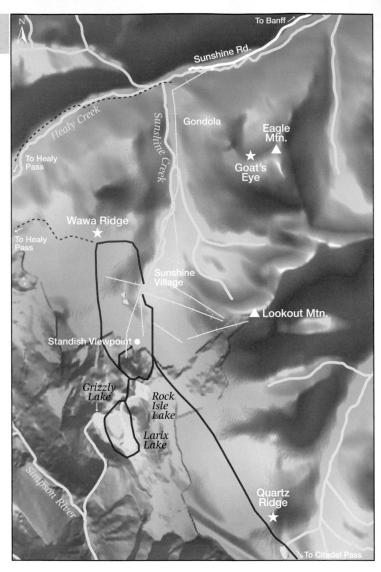

Grizzly Lake

Grizzly-Larix Lakes Loop

Length: 4.9 km (3.0 mi) roundtrip from Rock Isle Lake
Elevation loss: 65 m (220 ft)
Walking time: 1.5 hours roundtrip

While the trip to the Rock Isle Lake and back can be completed in little more than an hour, most hikers extend their outing by descending to Grizzly and Larix Lakes. Continuing beyond Rock Isle Lake, the trail drops into alpine larch and fir and incredibly lush wildflower meadows. Soon, the trail splits to begin a 2.5-kilometre (1.6-mile) loop around both lakes. Keep left to reach Larix (the botanical name for larch), the largest of the two lakes. You follow the shoreline for nearly one kilometre (0.6 miles) before the trail veers left and contours along the top of towering cliffs overlooking the Simpson River Valley. It then descends gradually through an open forest of larch to shallow Grizzly Lake. From this lake's inlet bridge, the trail climbs back to the loop split and returns to Rock Isle Lake.

Twin Cairns-Meadow Park

Length: 6.2 km (3.9 mi) roundtrip
Elevation gain: 210 m (690 ft)
Walking time: 2.5 hours roundtrip

Beyond Rock Isle Lake Viewpoint, the Grizzly-Larix Lakes Loop spurs left and this lofty trail heads uphill to the right. After a short climb, a 500-metre (0.3-mile) side-trail leads to a viewing platform near the top of Standish Ridge, from where there is an outstanding panorama of the Sunshine Meadows region. Wildflowers on this slope are exceptional throughout late July and early August. Back on the main trail, you climb gradually through an open meadow for nearly two kilometres (1.2 miles) to a junction atop Wawa Ridge, from where the descent to Sunshine Village is 1.6 kilometres (one mile).

Strong hikers can easily complete both the Grizzly-Larix Lakes and the Twin Cairns-Meadow Park Loops in time to catch the last bus of the day back to the parking lot. Including the detour to Standish Ridge, this combination of trails is 10.6 kilometres (6.6 miles) and takes three to four hours without stops.

The trail stays close to Larix Lake.

descending Quartz Ridge

Citadel Pass

Length: 9.3 km (5.8 mi) one way
Elevation gain: 195 m (640 ft)
Walking time: 3 hours one way

A sign leads the way to Quartz Ridge.

The trail to Citadel Pass is one of the most scenic trips from Sunshine Village, but due to its length usually less crowded than the trails described above. Starting from the 1.3-kilometre (0.8-mile) junction on the trail to Rock Isle Lake, it runs southeast along the Continental Divide, rolling up and down through the heart of the Sunshine Meadows. Highlights include some of the finest wildflower meadows in Banff National Park, remote Howard Douglas Lake, and frequent vistas of the rugged peaks of British Columbia to the south and west. Since the trip is long and the last shuttle bus of the day leaves in the late afternoon, many hikers only go as far as Quartz Ridge (5.2 kilometres/3.2 miles from Sunshine Village, the highest point on the trail and a good viewpoint for the southern reaches of the meadows.

Healy Pass

Avoiding the crowds of Sunshine Meadows

Length: 9.2 km (5.7 mi) one way
Elevation gain: 655 m (2,150 ft)
Walking time: 3 hours one way
Starting point: Sunshine Village parking lot, 9 km (5.6 mi) west of Banff on the Trans-Canada Hwy. then along the Sunshine Rd. for another 9 km (5.6 mi)
Origin of the name: Captain John Gerome Healy, a local prospector

DAY TRIP

Healy Pass and the extensive wildflower meadows beneath its summit might be considered a northerly extension of the nearby Sunshine Meadows. Though the hike to the pass and back via Healy Creek requires a full day, the open views and colourful snowbed flowers are ample reward.

Start from the far end of the parking lot at the base of the Sunshine Village gondola (look for a creekside trailhead kiosk behind the day lodge). The trail follows a wide track for 800 metres (0.5 miles)

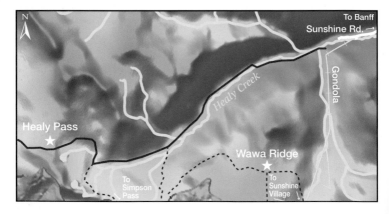

before branching right onto a more aesthetic forest path. Gradually but steadily, you climb the Healy Creek Valley, moving through Engelmann spruce and alpine fir to open subalpine meadows. The ascent culminates among the last scattered alpine larch on Healy Pass. This 2,330-meter-high (7,650-foot) depression on the Monarch Ramparts ridgeline is dominated by The Monarch, a distinctive pyramid-shaped peak to the south, with views westward into the lake-studded Egypt Lake district.

Healy Creek is your constant companion on this trail.

Options: As the Healy Pass trail emerges into Healy Meadows at km 7.7 (mi 4.8), a trail leading to Simpson Pass branches to the left. Follow this trail for two kilometres (1.2 miles) through open meadows and down through forest to the crest of Simpson Pass. From this point, the left fork leads back to the Healy Pass trail. A more scenic option from Simpson Pass is to walk 5.6 kilometres (3.5 miles) to Sunshine Village via Wawa Ridge on the Twin Cairns Meadow Park Trail (see page 76). From Sunshine Village, plan on catching a shuttle bus back to the parking lot (see *Transportation* under *Sources*).

The meadows at Healy Pass seemingly extend forever.

Arnica Lake

Two lakes for the price of one

Length: 5 km (3.1 mi) one way
Elevation gain: 580 m (1,900 ft), elevation loss 120 m (400 ft)
Walking time: 1.5 to 2 hours one way
Starting point: Hwy. 93, 8 km (5 mi) west of Castle Junction
Origin of the name: A descriptive name taken from the yellow flowers that grow near the lake

DAY TRIP

Vista Lake is a worthwhile destination in itself.

Arnica Lake is one of the more popular day hikes along the eastern escarpment of the Continental Divide. This despite the round-trip being quite grueling— another lake en route and open views from the slopes of Storm Mountain help to compensate for the workout.

Starting at unsigned Vista Lake Viewpoint, a narrow trail descends steadily through the silver spars of trees killed by a forest fire that swept Vermilion Pass in 1968. It soon reaches its lowest elevation beside **Vista Lake**, a peaceful green body of water that is a pleasant destination for less energetic hikers. You will want to spend some time here relaxing and enjoying the scene before tackling the steep climb ahead.

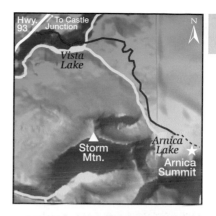

From the lake's outlet bridge, the trail climbs eastward through a dense forest of lodgepole pine across the lower slopes of Storm Mountain. Four kilometres (2.5 miles) from the trailhead, you leave the burn and enter a mature subalpine forest. After passing a small pond, the trail reaches Arnica Lake. Backed against the sheer eastern face of Storm Mountain, the lake is enclosed on three sides by a forest of Engelmann spruce, alpine fir, and larch. The lake's namesake, the yellow-flowered arnica, is found throughout this cool, moist forest during early summer.

Options: From the lake's outlet, a trail climbs for 800 metres (0.5 mile) to **Arnica Summit**, where you are rewarded with extensive views north and south along the Bow Valley.

The trail is named for yellow arnicas, which are common around the lake.

Taylor Lake

Lakeside solitude in a glacially carved valley

Length: 6.3 km (3.9 mi) one way
Elevation gain: 585 m (1,920 ft)
Walking time: 2 to 2.5 hours one way
Starting point: Trans-Canada Hwy., 8 km (5 mi) west of Castle Junction and 17 km (10.5 mi) east of Lake Louise
Origin of the name: George Herbert Taylor, a packer on an early surveying expedition

DAY TRIP

Taylor Lake is set in a classic hanging valley high on the western slope of the Bow Valley—a scenic destination that can be reached in two hours. This trail also offers the bonus of attractive side-trips to nearby O'Brien Lake and the meadows and larch forests of Panorama Meadows.

The hike to the lake is straightforward though not particularly scenic as it switchbacks up the side of the valley through a closed forest of pine and spruce. The goal is well worth the drudgery of the climb, however, when the broad, often-muddy trail suddenly emerges into a meadow below the lake's outlet—a moist area carpeted with western anemone, marsh marigold, buttercups, and mountain laurel throughout much of the summer. Though the lake is bordered by dense, subalpine forest, the rugged cliffs of Mount Bell provide a dramatic backdrop above its southern and western shore.

Just before reaching Taylor Lake, the trail crosses Taylor Creek.

Options: O'Brien Lake lies in a small cirque 2.1 kilometres (1.2 miles) to the south of Taylor Lake. With a lavish display of wildflowers along its shore and alpine larch in the surrounding forest, it is a

Taylor Lake

worthwhile side-trip from Taylor. To reach the lake, cross Taylor Creek just below Taylor Lake and follow a rocky trail that descends beneath Mount Bell's cliffs and then climbs to O'Brien's outlet stream. Follow a muddy, sometimes vague trail upstream to the lake. From a short way along the north shoreline of Taylor Lake, the trail to **Panorama Meadows** climbs for 500 metres (0.3 miles) to one of the great wildflower meadows and larch forests in Banff National Park.

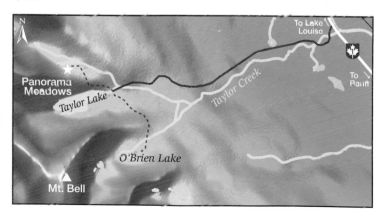

Shadow Lake

An overnight in the wilderness

Length: 14 km (8.7 mi) one way
Elevation gain: 440 m (1,450 ft)
Walking time: 4 to 5 hours one way
Starting point: Trans-Canada Hwy., 20 km (12.5 mi) west of Banff and 10.5 km (6.5 mi) east of Castle Junction
Origin of the name: This lake lies in the shadow of Mt. Ball

OVERNIGHT

Shadow Lake stretches out beneath the massive cliffs of Mount Ball and is one of the most remote lakes along the western slope of the Bow Valley. Fit hikers reach the lake and return in a single day, while others come equipped for backcountry camping. But the option that makes the least demand on your legs and back is to make reservations at **Shadow Lake Lodge**, where meals and comfortable beds are provided (see *Accommodations* under *Sources*).

Shadow Lake Lodge

Much of the journey to the lake follows the broad track of an old roadbed. The hiking is somewhat tedious, but the climb is gradual and it is easy to make good time. After 10.5 kilometres (6.5 miles), the trail branches right from the road and continues up-valley

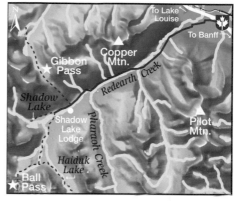

as a standard-width, forest path. (Mountain bikes are permitted as far as this junction.) From this point, it's 2.4 kilometres (1.5 miles) to the lodge and 3.5 kilometres (2.2 miles) to the lake. Stretching for two kilometers (1.2 miles), Shadow Lake is large compared with most subalpine lakes, and at 3,311 metres (10,862 feet) Mount Ball is the highest mountain between Mount Assiniboine, to the south, and Mount Temple, near Lake Louise.

Options: If you spend two nights at the lodge, you have a full day to explore the area. Trail accessible destinations include the north shore of Shadow Lake (3.0 km/1.9 mi), the wildflower meadows of **Gibbon Pass** (3.1 km/2 mi), the lofty mountain views from **Ball Pass** (8.1 km/5 mi), and the dramatic surroundings of **Haiduk Lake** (8.1 km/5 mi). All distances are one-way from Shadow Lake Lodge.

¹ signposted as Red Earth Creek

Wildflowers are a major attraction for hikers heading to Shadow Lake.

Lake Louise/Moraine Lake

Simply put, there are few hiking areas in the world that can rival the Lake Louise/Moraine Lake region. These two lakes, stunning destinations themselves, provide the starting point for a great variety of trails leading through some of the most rugged yet accessible alpine scenery imaginable. The most popular destination from Lake Louise is Lake Agnes, where a rustic teahouse serves hungry hikers, while Larch Valley is the target for adventurous Moraine Lake visitors.

Lake Louise

Bow River Loop

Linking the village of Lake Louise

Length: 7.1 km (4.4 mi) roundtrip
Elevation gain: minimal
Walking time: 2 hours roundtrip
Starting point: North end of Sentinel Rd., village of Lake Louise
Origin of the name: Reeds along the Bow River were used by native people to make bows

SHORT WALK

This pleasant loop trail along the banks of the Bow River can be accessed from various points throughout the village of Lake Louise, including behind Samson Mall and either of the campgrounds. We give the starting point as the north end of Sentinel Road as there is ample parking, a trailhead kiosk, and delicious lunches at the adjacent Station Restaurant.

The trail never strays far from the Bow River.

From Sentinel Road, either head downstream along the east side of the river or cross the footbridge and follow the west side. Whichever route you choose, the trail follows the river for approximately 3.5 kilometres (2.2 miles), with the option to shorten the roundtrip distance to two kilometres (1.2 miles) by crossing the river on the Lake Louise Drive bridge or four kilometres (2.5 miles) by crossing the campground bridge. Regardless of which option taken, you'll never be far from the clear, rushing waters of the Bow River, its banks lined with colorful flowers in summer and views extending north to the Waputik Range.

Options: Between 1913 and 1930, before a road was built between the valley floor and Lake Louise, visitors were transported from the railway station on a tram. Today, the tracks have long gone, but the railbed remains as the **Lake Louise Tramline**, a pleasant walking trail that climbs 210 vertical meters (690 feet) over 4.5 kilometres (2.8 miles). From the north end of Sentinel Road, the trail crosses the Bow River and comes in sight of Lake Louise Drive after 1.6 kilometres (one mile), then turns right along Louise Creek and switchbacks to the left across Lake Louise Drive and Moraine Lake Road before making the final ascent to Lake Louise. The Tramline Trail is crossed by the 2.7-kilometre (1.7-mile) **Louise Creek Trail**, which takes a more direct route to the lake from the south side of the road bridge across the Bow River.

Spoil yourself with lunch at the Station Restaurant after completing this walk.

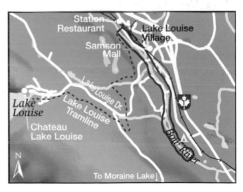

Lake Louise Lakeshore

Walk into one of the world's most famous landscapes

Length: 1.9 km (1.2 mi) one way
Elevation gain: minimal
Walking time: 30 minutes one way
Starting point: In front of the Chateau Lake Louise
Origin of the name: Princess Louise, 4th daughter of Queen Victoria

EASY WALK

Believe it or not, you can walk to the far end of Lake Louise and back on the very popular lakeshore trail and not meet another soul (we've done it in the late evening in early spring). Yet, even

One of the park's most scenic trails, the walk along Lake Louise is accessible to everyone.

when it's busy, there are worse ways to spend an hour than strolling along this broad, flat trail with its ever-changing views of great peaks.

The walk officially starts from just beyond the Chateau and follows along the north shoreline to where the silt-laden waters from the Victoria Glacier feed into the lake. Away from the crowds in front of the hotel, you can better appreciate the description by British mountaineer James Outram shortly after the turn of the 20th century: "At every season,

looking back down the lake to the Chateau Lake Louise

every hour, it is wonderful....
As a gem of composition and of
colouring it is perhaps unrivalled
anywhere."

At the far end of the lake the
trail climbs over a low rise and
traverses beneath quartzite
cliffs, which are often decorated
by the colourful ropes of Lycra-
clad rock climbers. And if you sit

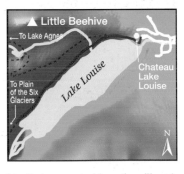

down to have a snack, you'll undoubtedly be greeted by other "head-
of-the-lake" inhabitants, including golden-mantled ground squirrels,
least chipmunks, Clark's nutcrackers, and grey jays. Back across the
lake, the Chateau floats on the distant shore with the slopes of the
local alpine resort visible on the distant mountains. It's enough to
make a person want to keep on hiking. (See *Plain of the Six Glaciers*,
page 106).

Moraine Lakeshore

A stroll beneath the Ten Peaks

Length: 1.2 km (0.7 mi) one way
Elevation gain: minimal
Walking time: 20 minutes one way
Starting point: The end of Moraine Lake Rd., 12.5 km (7.5 mi) from
Lake Louise Dr.
Origin of the name: Misnamed for what was thought by early explorers to
be glacial debris at the lake's outlet

EASY WALK

In 1899, Walter Wilcox and Ross Peacock set out to explore the lower reaches of "Desolation Valley," which Wilcox had surveyed and named from the summit of Mount Temple five years earlier. (His party could only see the massive rockslides at the head of the valley from the summit and hence the name Desolation.) After a

Moraine Lake

hard bushwhack into the valley, Wilcox came to a "massive pile of stones" blocking the way ahead. He climbed to the top and, behold, "there lay before me one of the most beautiful lakes that I have ever seen."

Beyond the oft-photographed canoe dock, the Moraine Lakeshore trail transports you away from the crowds milling about the parking lot, lodge, and viewpoint, allowing for peaceful appreciation of what many visitors feel is one of the most beautiful lakes they've ever seen. The trail remains flat and close to the shoreline all the way to the lake's inlet at its southwest end. Along the way, you have continuous views across the lake to the rugged summits of the first five of the Ten Peaks rising from its eastern shore. Most impressive is Mount Fay, with its prominent summit glacier.

Options: To get the top of the "massive pile of stones" noted by Wilcox, follow the trail leading downhill from beside the parking lot washrooms. Known as the **Rockpile Trail**, it climbs around the back of a rockslide to emerge at a viewpoint that provides the classic view of the lake.

Climb to the top of the Rockpile for this classic view of the lake.

Lake Agnes

High tea amid high peaks

Length: 3.5 km (2.2 mi) one way
Elevation gain: 400 m (1,300 ft)
Walking time: 1 to 1.5 hours one way
Starting point: In front of the Chateau Lake Louise
Origin of the name: Lady Susan Agnes MacDonald, wife of Canada's first Prime Minister

SHORT HIKE

Lake Agnes is hidden in a hanging valley high above Lake Louise. In addition to its own charms, which include a teahouse, the two Beehives provide breathtaking views of Lake Louise and a broad stretch of the Bow Valley.

As you walk along the shoreline of Lake Louise, the trail to Lake Agnes branches right just beyond the hotel, then climbs steadily

Mirror Lake

Lake Agnes

through dense subalpine forest. After 1.7 kilometres (1.1 miles), the first switchback marks a break in the trees where you have a clear view down to the pale turquoise water of Lake Louise. Another one kilometre (0.6 miles) of forest-enclosed climbing brings you to **Mirror Lake**, a tiny lake with dark, layered cliffs of the Big Beehive looming above. The two trails leading off in opposite directions from Mirror Lake both converge at Lake Agnes; the left option is slightly shorter and steeper than the traditional route to the right. Regardless of which route you choose, the final climb to Lake Agnes is completed on one of two steep, wooden staircases, which surmount a cliff band beside a waterfall created by the lake's outlet stream. Arriving at the narrow opening where Lake Agnes tumbles from its basin, the lake appears in its entirety, stretching westward to a jagged mountain backdrop.

The original Lake Agnes Teahouse was constructed in the early 1900s. The present-day version was built in 1981. It serves refreshments and light snacks from mid-June to early October and is one of the big attractions for many who do this hike. While its covered balcony is a relaxing place to sit and admire the view, it is usually very busy. The

Lake Agnes Teahouse

area surrounding Lake Agnes abounds with wildlife of the upper subalpine forest, especially those species who like to be where people are eating. Least chipmunks, golden-mantled ground squirrels, Clark's nutcrackers, and grey jays congregate around the teahouse looking for an easy meal. Marmots and pikas, who whistle and cheep from the rocky slopes above the lakeshore, are somewhat less corrupted by humanity.

Options: The most popular short hike beyond Lake Agnes is to **Little Beehive**, which provides an excellent panorama of the Bow River stretching from the mountains near its headwaters to surrounding peaks around the town of Banff to the south. Between Lake Agnes and Little Beehive are a number of rocky viewpoints overlooking Lake Louise, the hanging valley containing Lake Agnes, and Mount Aberdeen and the glacier-crowned peaks of Mounts Lefroy and Victoria. This 0.9-kilometre (0.6-mile) trail branches uphill from the shore of Lake Agnes just beyond the teahouse.

From the teahouse, it takes around 15 minutes to reach the western end of Lake Agnes, where a rough trail switchbacks up a ridge.

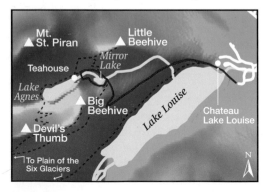

Traverse eastward (take the left fork) along the ridge's rocky spine to a gazebo-style shelter at the top of **Big Beehive**. Though somewhat obscured by trees, there are views over the Bow

from the Little Beehive, Lake Louise spreads out below

Valley and down to Lake Louise, over 500 vertical metres (1,640 feet) below. Total distance between the teahouse and Big Beehive is 1.6 kilometres (one mile); allow 40 minutes one way. (Do not attempt to shortcut down from the gazebo viewpoint in any direction; there are dangerous cliffs on all sides. Return back along the ridge the way you came.)

Hikers looking for a full day's outing can include the **Plain of the Six Glaciers** in their itinerary after visiting Lake Agnes by crossing the Big Beehive's summit ridge and descending steeply for one kilometre (0.6 miles) to a trail running up-valley from Mirror Lake. Turn right and follow this trail as it descends across the lower slopes of Devil's Thumb to an intersection with the Plain of the Six Glaciers trail (see page 106). Continue up-valley toward the imposing, glacier-topped summits of Mounts Lefroy and Victoria for another 1.4 kilometres (0.9 miles) to the Plain of the Six Glaciers Teahouse. Total distance for this combination of trails, without detours to the either of the Beehives, is 13.6 kilometres (8.5 miles) and you will have gained and lost almost 800 metres (2,620 feet); allow at five or six hours.

Fairview Lookout

More than just a fair view

Length: 1.4 km (0.9 mi) one way
Elevation gain: 140 m (460 ft)
Walking time: 30 minutes one way
Starting point: behind the boathouse, Lake Louise
Origin of the name: A descriptive name

SHORT HIKE

The trail starts at the boathouse.

Everyone who visits Lake Louise photographs the Chateau Lake Louise from one angle or another. Yet, one of the better vantage points is from the Fairview Lookout—a view that takes in both the hotel and the Bow Valley beyond. The trail is short, moderately steep, and usually not that busy.

Following the paved shoreline trail in front of the Chateau Lake Louise, walk toward the boathouse and pick up the trail as it disappears into the forest. After 400 metres (0.2 miles), a trailhead kiosk is reached. This is the junction for Saddleback (see page 108), which lies straight ahead. Take the right fork and follow a broad, smooth track that climbs steadily through the cool Engelmann spruce-alpine fir forest.

The view of Chateau Lake Louise and the east end of the lake from the wooden observation platform at the top is partially obscured by trees, but interpretive boards describe the history of the hotel and its stunning location. Most hikers return the way they came, but a rough, muddy trail does descend steeply from the platform to the boathouse.

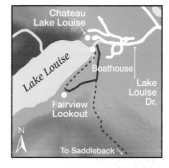

looking down to Lake Louise from Fairview Lookout

Larch Valley

The wonderful world of larch

Length: 2.4 km (1.5 mi) one way
Elevation gain: 350 m (1,150 ft)
Walking time: 1 hour one way
Starting point: The end of Moraine Lake Rd., 12.5 km (7.5 mi) from Lake Louise Dr.
Origin of the name: A descriptive name for alpine larch at the lower end of the valley

SHORT HIKE

Larch Valley is one of the most heavily visited hiking destinations in the Canadian Rockies. And no wonder. This meadowland above Moraine Lake, with its dense stands of alpine larch and panoramic overview of the Valley of the Ten Peaks, is exquisite. Although the valley can be reached in an hour (which is why we've classed it as a Short Hike), it's easy to spend a full day exploring the surrounding area.

Larch Valley is renowned for its fall display of golden-coloured larch.

From the canoe dock at Moraine Lake, the trail passes the trailhead kiosk and climbs through a forest of Engelmann spruce and alpine fir, steadily ascending switchbacks much of the way. Stay right at the km 2.4 (mi 1.5) junction and immediately enter the lower meadows of Larch Valley. This high valley is the main focus for most hikers, and in late September, when alpine larch needles have turned to gold, it is especially popular. In mid-summer, however, the larch needles are pale green and the meadows are carpeted with wildflowers.

The trail continues to climb through larch groves and meadows, and by the time it emerges above the last trees, there are fine views back to the rugged Ten Peaks—the glacier-capped summit of Mount Fay being the most prominent and striking.

Many small streams flow through the valley.

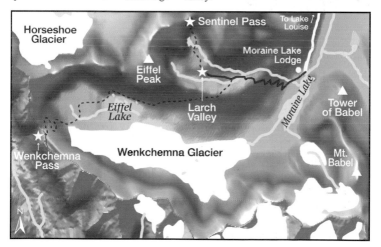

Lower Minnestimma Lake, with Mt. Fay in the distance

Small lakes that dot the upper meadows of the valley are called *Minnestimma*, a native word meaning "sleeping water."

Options: Sentinel Pass is an obvious but strenuous extension from the upper Larch Valley and the last of the Minnestimma Lakes. The trail begins a switchbacking climb of the steep, open slope leading to the pass—a vertical rise of nearly 200 metres (660 feet). At 2,611 metres (8,560 feet), Sentinel is one of the highest trail-accessible passes in the Rockies. Distinctive rock towers give the pass its name and views back over Larch Valley to the Ten Peaks are breathtaking. Total one way distance to the pass from Moraine Lake is 5.8 kilometres (3.6 miles).

Eiffel Lake is an easier option than the climb to Sentinel Pass. Beginning where the Larch Valley trail first enters the meadows, it runs along the north side of the Valley of the Ten Peaks and soon emerges onto open slopes where all of the ten summits are revealed across the valley. At km 5.6 (mi 3.5) the trail passes across a scree slope above Eiffel Lake, which was aptly described by Walter Wilcox over a century ago: "It would be difficult to find another lake of small size in a wilder setting, the shores being of great angular stones, perfectly in harmony with the wild range of mountains beyond. Except in one place where a green and inviting slope comes down to the water, this rough ground is utterly unsuitable for vegetation and nearly devoid of trees." If you don't want to labour down broken rock to reach Eiffel Lake, enjoy an overview of both lake and the Ten Peaks by continuing west along the trail to a sheltering grove of larch—Wilcox's "green and inviting slope."

You can hike beyond Eiffel Lake for another four kilometres (2.5 miles) to 2,600-metre-high (8,530-foot) **Wenkchemna Pass**, another one of the highest trail-accessible passes in the Canadian Rockies and yet another outstanding viewpoint for the Valley of the Ten Peaks. This trail continues west from the Eiffel Lake viewpoint across rolling alpine meadows, then climbs over a moraine and along the rocky south ridge of Wenkchemna Peak before descending to the windswept gap between Wenkchemna Peak and Neptuak Mountain. The pass is 9.7 kilometres (6.2 miles) from Moraine Lake; you should allow three to four hours one way.

Note: Travel in Larch Valley and to Eiffel Lake may require a group of four people hiking in close proximity to one another if restrictions concerning grizzly bears are in place.

Eiffel Lake

Consolation Lakes

Escape the crowded shore of Moraine Lake

Length: 2.9 km (1.8 mi) one way
Elevation gain: 65 m (215 ft)
Walking time: under 1 hour one way
Starting point: Moraine Creek, below the public washrooms at Moraine Lake parking area
Origin of the name: Explorer Walter Wilcox saw the lake as a contrasting consolation to adjacent "Desolation Valley"

SHORT HIKE

Created by the massive rockslides from Mount Babel and backed by the distinctive, glacier-draped summits of Bident and Quadra Mountains, Lower Consolation Lake is a scenic destination that can be reached in less than hour over mainly flat trail from Moraine Lake.

After crossing Moraine Creek, the trail passes over a substantial rockslide that created Moraine Lake. (A short trail branches to the top of the Rockpile, revealing the classic view of Moraine Lake and the Valley of the Ten Peaks.) Beyond the rockslide, the trail continues into the forest and climbs gradually beside Babel Creek. Just over halfway to the lake, the trail levels out along a meadow (a section that is often quite muddy).

A rockslide blocks direct access to the north end of Lower Consolation Lake, but you can scramble across the large boulders for a relaxed view of the lake and the glacier-capped summits of Bident and Quadra beyond. Mount Temple, at 3,544

one of many streams flowing into Babel Creek

metres (11,630 feet) the third highest mountain in Banff National Park, commands the view back down-valley to the north.

Options: If you want to spend a little more time in the area and are well shod, consider a visit to **Upper Consolation Lake**. Cross Babel Creek below Lower Consolation Lake on rickety log booms, then follow a rough, muddy track along the lake's eastern shore. At the far end, climb over a ridge of rock debris separating the two lakes. Allow 30 minutes one way from the creek crossing.

Note: Travel to Consolation Lakes may require a group of four people hiking in close proximity to one another if special restrictions concerning grizzly bears are in place.

Lower Consolation Lake

Plain of the Six Glaciers

Glorious glaciers

Length: 5.5 km (3.4 mi) one way
Elevation gain: 340 m (1,110 ft)
Walking time: 1.5 to 2 hours one way
Starting point: In front of the Chateau Lake Louise
Origin of the name: A descriptive name

DAY TRIP

The Plain of the Six Glaciers Trail transports hikers into the heart of Canada's most famous postcard view, deposits them at the foot of two of the park's highest mountains and, as the name suggests, is surrounded by glaciers. And if all this scenery weren't enough, you can enjoy refreshments at an historic backcountry teahouse.

looking west toward Mt. Victoria from the teahouse

Follow the busy Lake Louise Lakeshore Trail (see page 90) to the far end of lake. Beyond the lake's inlet, the trail begins its steady climb through a subalpine forest laced with avalanche paths. Eventually it emerges into a massive basin holding the Victoria Glacier, where views open to the two glacier-capped giants, Mounts Victoria (3,464 m/11,370 ft) and Lefroy (3,441

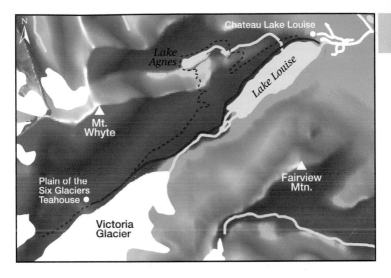

m/11,290 ft). After passing along a cliff, a series of switchbacks lead up to a meadow bordered by alpine fir and larch 5.5 kilometres (3.4 miles) from the trailhead. A small area of the meadow has been landscaped with benches and stone pathways, while off to the right is the Plain of the Six Glaciers Teahouse, which has been serving light snacks to hungry hikers for over 80 years. For the full effect, talk your way to a table on the upstairs verandah.

Options: From the teahouse, a trail continues up-valley 1.6 kilometres (one mile), traversing the sharp crest of a lateral moraine to a rocky slope overlooking the boulder-covered ice of the Victoria Glacier and the couloir leading to Abbot Pass.

An option for strong hikers is returning to Lake Louise via Lake Agnes (see page 94). Descending from the Plain of the Six Glaciers, take the signposted left fork 1.4 kilometres (0.9 miles) from the teahouse. At the next junction, branch left and climb over the Big Beehive to Lake Agnes. It is a strenuous trip, and the total roundtrip distance from Lake Louise is 15 kilometres (9.3 miles). Allow five or six hours.

Saddleback

The wild side of Lake Louise

Length: 3.7 km (2.3 mi) one way
Elevation gain: 600 m (1,970 ft)
Walking time: 1.5 hours one way
Starting point: behind the boathouse, Lake Louise
Origin of the name: A descriptive name for the saddle-shaped pass

DAY TRIP

This steep trail ends at a 2,330-metre-high (7,650-foot) pass set between Saddle Peak and Fairview Mountain. Alpine meadows at the summit are filled with flowers through much of the summer and views stretch out over Paradise Valley to Mount Temple's north wall. In late September, the needles on giant larch trees just beneath the pass turn gold, making it a popular destination for hikers in search of fall colour.

From the Lake Louise boathouse, the trail enters the forest and follows along the same path as the trail to Fairview Lookout (see page 98) for 400 metres (0.2 mile). Continue straight ahead at the trailhead kiosk. After one kilometre (0.6 miles), the trail crosses an avalanche path, allowing unimpeded views back to the Chateau and distant Mount Hector. Farther along, the trail angles southwest and begins the final steep, switchbacking ascent to the pass. Views over the Bow Valley improve just below the summit, where the trail passes through a stand of unusually large—and probably very old—alpine larch.

Saddleback is a pleasant upland meadow where flowers like buttercups, western anemone, white mountain avens and alpine speedwell are the first to appear after the snow disappears in early summer. The best views of Mount Temple, tiny Lake Annette, and Paradise Valley are obtained by descending southeast (left from the

looking across Sheol Valley from Saddleback

pass) approximately 300 metres (0.2 miles) through a thick cover of scrubby alpine fir to a rocky promontory overlooking Sheol Valley.

Options: When the weather allows, many strong hikers climb north from Saddleback to the 2,745-metre-high (9,000-foot) summit of **Fairview Mountain**. A rough 1.3-kilometre (0.8-mile) path leads to the mountaintop, which provides a true alpine experience and a panoramic

view of Mount Victoria, Mount Temple, Sheol Mountain, and the turquoise waters of Lake Louise a vertical kilometre (3,280 feet) below.

Paradise Valley

Hiking through paradise

Length: 5.7 km (3.5 mi) one-way to Lake Annette
Elevation gain: 600 m (1,970 ft)
Walking time: 2 hours one way
Starting point: Moraine Lake Rd., 2.5 km (1.5 mi) from Lake Louise Dr.
Origin of the name: A descriptive name bestowed by Walter Wilcox in 1894

DAY TRIP

When Walter Wilcox and his companions climbed to Mitre Pass from Lake Louise in 1894, they looked into "a valley of surpassing beauty, wide and beautiful, with alternating open meadows and rich forests." They named it Paradise.

While it's possible to hike to the Giant Steps and back in a long day, most hikers opt for the more modest and scenic objective of **Lake Annette**, nestled beneath the awe-inspiring north wall of Mount Temple. The first three kilometres (1.9 miles) of trail are forest-enclosed, but at the first Paradise Creek bridge, views open to Mount Temple. In another one kilometre (0.6 miles), the trail crosses back to the northwest side of the creek. At km 5.1 (mi 3.2), the trail crosses the creek once

an avalanche thunders off Mount Temple, with Lake Annette in the foreground

more followed by a short but strenuous ascent to Lake Annette. Annette's rocky surroundings are typical of many subalpine lakes, but its backdrop is extraordinary—the north face of Mount Temple rises dramatically 1,200 metres (3,940 feet) above the lake. This

wall is one of the most difficult ascents in North America and remained unclimbed until 1966. And if you see one of the massive avalanches that sweep the face, you will understand one reason why.

Options: The trail continues southwest from Lake Annette, climbing through stands of alpine larch to a summit atop a major rockslide. Here views open to the valley headwall—scenery that is blithely ignored by the marmots and pikas inhabiting the surrounding boulder field. Strong hikers may want to continue beyond this viewpoint

Giant Steps

to **Giant Steps**, a staircase waterfall 10.3 kilometres (6.4 miles) from the trailhead.

Note: Travel in Paradise Valley may require a group of four people hiking in close proximity to one another if restrictions concerning grizzly bears are in place.

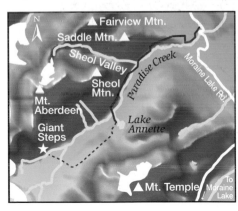

Skoki Valley

Day hiking from a historic lodge

Length: 14.4 km (8.9 mi) one way to Skoki Lodge
Elevation gain: 785 m (2,575 ft), elevation loss 310 m (1,020 ft)
Walking time: 4 to 5 hours one way
Starting point: Fish Creek Parking Lot, off Whitehorn Rd. uphill toward the Lake Louise ski area
Origin of the name: A native word that translates to "swamp"

OVERNIGHT

Hidden behind the Lake Louise ski area is Skoki Valley—one of the exceptional hiking areas in the Canadian Rockies. Strong day hikers can travel as far as Boulder Pass and Ptarmigan Lake (8.6 km/5.3 miles from the trailhead) and return in six or seven hours, but to fully immerse yourself in the setting, make reservations at historic

Marmots are common throughout this high alpine region.

Skoki Lodge

Skoki Lodge (see *Accommodations* under *Sources*), where rates include accommodation, meals, and the local knowledge of friendly hosts.

Those with lodge reservations are transported by van from the Fish Creek Parking Lot to the ski area's Temple Day Lodge, a four-kilometre (2.5-mile) stretch of unremarkable service road that day hikers must traverse on foot. (The shuttle service for guests decreases the hiking time quoted above by one hour). From this point, the road reverts to trail, climbing steeply across a ski run and into a pleasant subalpine forest of spruce and alpine fir with a scattering of larch. From the meadow 2.4 kilometres (1.5 miles) beyond Temple Day Lodge, views ahead extend to Boulder Pass and the rugged mountains that form the core of the Slate Range. A further one kilometre (0.6 miles) of walking brings you to the Halfway Hut shelter, which was originally built in the 1930s to serve skiers bound for Skoki Lodge.

Beyond Halfway Hut, the trail climbs through scattered forest to the summit of Boulder Pass and the west end of Ptarmigan Lake. At

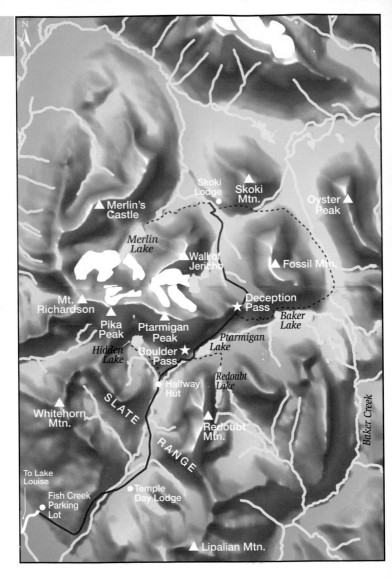

an elevation of 2,345 metres (7,700 feet), this lake-filled pass is at the upper limits of tree growth. The trail continues along the slopes above the north shore of Ptarmigan Lake and then climbs steadily to Deception Pass. Standing atop this 2,474-metre-high (8,120-foot) pass, there's an all-encompassing view back over the Ptarmigan Valley to Redoubt Mountain and through Boulder Pass to the distant mountains above Lake Louise. From Deception Pass, the trail drops steadily northward towards the Skoki Valley, reaching the lodge 3.4 kilometres (2.1 miles) beyond the pass.

Options: While the main trail into Skoki Valley is scenic, it is just a taste of the day-hiking possibilities for those staying at Skoki Lodge. Ideally, you should book two or three nights accommodation, allowing one or two full days to explore the region.

From the lodge it's 3.1 kilometres (1.9 miles) to **Merlin Lake**. Set between the colourfully named Wall of Jericho and Merlin's Castle, the lake is one of the little-known gems of Banff National Park. From

Merlin Lake

the front of Skoki Lodge, the trail crosses high boulder-fields before passing above Castilleja Lake and then ascending the cliff immediately below Merlin Lake. (Keep a close eye on rock cairns that lead to the cliff and ascend it by choosing the line of least resistance via the scree gully on the left side—a steep scramble over loose rock.) From the top of the cliff, the trail descends through meadow and stunted trees to the lakeshore.

Most popular of the various day hiking options from Skoki Lodge is the 13.4-kilometre (8.3-mile) **Fossil Mountain Circuit**. As the name suggests, this route circumnavigates Fossil Mountain. The first stretch retraces the route into the lodge over Deception Pass, branching left at a junction 0.5 kilometres (0.3 miles) below the pass for a short descent to Baker Lake. The trail follows this lake's northern shore for one kilometre (0.6 miles), staying left at a junction just east of Baker Lake Campground, and descends northeast gradually for one kilometre (0.6 miles) to the open meadows of Cotton Grass Pass. The trail continues north through the pass for a similar distance, passing beneath the steep eastern slopes of Fossil Mountain to a junction where the trail to Skoki Valley branches left and runs between Fossil and Skoki Mountains back to the lodge.

Both day hikers and lodge guests returning to civilization can detour to small lakes near Boulder Pass. **Redoubt Lake** is hidden in a basin just above Ptarmigan Lake, beneath the east-facing cliffs of Redoubt Mountain. The 1.1-kilometre (0.7-mile) side-trip begins at the west end of Ptarmigan Lake and follows the south shore as a rough, ill-defined track for 800 metres (0.5 miles), before climbing up to an obvious gap between Redoubt Mountain and Heather Ridge. From Redoubt Lake's outlet, you have a fine overview of larch forest, lush meadows, and Baker Creek Valley.

The 1.3-kilometre (0.8-mile) **Hidden Lake** trail branches north from the main trail just north of Halfway Hut. It climbs steadily to this small lake, which lies beneath Mount Richardson, Pika Peak, and Ptarmigan Peak and is surrounded by some of the finest wildflower meadows in the park.

Hidden Lake is a hidden gem.

Icefields Parkway

The 230-kilometre-long (143-mile) Icefields Parkway between Lake Louise and Jasper is undeniably one of Canada's most scenic highways. More importantly for outdoor enthusiasts, it is the highest stretch of road in Canada, allowing hikers to reach the treeless alpine a lot quicker than elsewhere in the park, most notably at Bow Summit and Parker Ridge. Backcountry lakes, alpine meadows, and photogenic waterfalls add to the appeal for those planning on leaving the blacktop behind.

Bow Lake, from along Bow Glacier Falls Trail

Mistaya Canyon

The amazing power of water

Length: 500 metres (0.3 mi) one way
Elevation loss: 40 m (130 ft)
Walking time: 10 minutes one way
Starting point: Icefields Parkway, 71.5 km (44 mi) north of the Trans-Canada Hwy. and 5.5 km (3.5 mi) south of Saskatchewan River Crossing
Origin of the name: A native word that translates to "bear"

EASY WALK

Hidden just below the Icefields Parkway, Mistaya is the least-known of the mountain parks' limestone slot canyons. That makes it one of the most enjoyable to visit since you won't have to cope with the crowds found at Johnston and other canyons.

looking downstream toward the bridge

Follow a broad track downhill through forest for 10 minutes to reach the canyon, which was carved from limestone

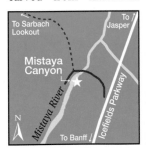

Water from the Mistaya River is forced through a narrow canyon.

bedrock by the swiftly flowing Mistaya River. From a bridge spanning the canyon at its narrowest point, you can peer down into its dark depths. The river flows through willow meadows upstream from the bridge, and rock slabs near the point where it plunges into the abyss are a pleasant place to relax and enjoy the upstream view. Avoid the temptation of peering into the canyon from anywhere except the bridge. Unfenced, canyon-rim viewpoints can be very dangerous, particularly when conditions underfoot are wet, icy, or snowy.

Options: A trail climbs into the forest beyond the canyon bridge, then quickly branches left and climbs steadily for 4.7 kilometres (2.9 miles) to **Sarbach Lookout**. Views at the top are mostly obscured by trees, but if you are willing to scramble up-slope for another 45 minutes or so, there is a panorama encompassing the confluence of three rivers and a sea of massive peaks and glaciers. The trail gains 595 metres (1,950 feet) of elevation, so you should allow up to two hours one way.

Bow Glacier Falls

Visit the source of the Bow River

Length: 4.7 km (2.9 mi) one way
Elevation gain: 95 m (310 ft)
Walking time: 1.5 hours one way
Starting point: Num-Ti-Jah Lodge, 36 km (22.5 mi) north along the Icefields Parkway from the Trans-Canada Hwy.
Origin of the name: Reeds along the Bow River were used by native people to make bows

SHORT HIKE

Bow Glacier has been a popular half-day hike for travellers ever since the tourist-explorer Walter Wilcox visited it in 1896. The glacier, which was much larger in Wilcox's day, has retreated above the headwall, leaving a 120-metre-high (400-foot) waterfall as the only hint of the icefield hidden above.

Crowfoot Mountain rises majestically across Bow Lake

Bow Lake has to be one of the finest places to start a hike along the Icefields Parkway. From the parking lot, the trail skirts along the lakeshore and passes historic Num-Ti-Jah Lodge. After crossing willow flats beyond the lodge, it continues beside the lake's northern shoreline. Views over this first two-kilometre (1.2-mile) stretch extend across turquoise-coloured waters to Crowfoot Mountain and the leaning spire of Mount St. Nicholas rising from the white expanse of the Wapta Glacier. The trail beyond the lake is mainly flat and follows near the silty, glacier-fed steam draining the basin. One kilometre (0.6 miles) beyond the lake, the trail climbs steeply along the rim of a narrow gorge (hazardous when wet, icy, or snowcovered). As described by Wilcox: "Where the canyon is deepest an immense block of limestone about twenty-five feet long has fallen down, and with either end resting on the canyon walls, it affords a natural bridge over the gloomy chasm."

the final approach to Bow Glacier Falls

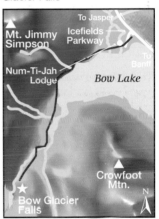

Fortunately, the trail does not cross the hazardous natural bridge, but continues up along the gorge to the sparsely forested crest of a terminal moraine. From this viewpoint, the glacially-carved basin lies below and Bow Glacier Falls pours off the headwall beyond. The trail continues another one kilometre (0.6 miles) across the rocky basin to the base of the waterfall, which is most impressive during the warmest days of summer.

Bow Summit Lookout

A short climb to the alpine

Length: 3.1 km (1.9 mi) one way
Elevation gain: 230 m (760 ft)
Walking time: 1 hour one way
Starting point: Bow Summit, 41 km (25.5 mi) north along the Icefields Parkway from the Trans-Canada Hwy.
Origin of the name: Reeds along the Bow River were used by native people to make bows

SHORT HIKE

Many thousands of people walk the paved nature trail to the Peyto Lake viewing platform every summer. This short, uphill trek provides Icefields Parkway travellers with an excuse to stretch their legs and take turns photographing the turquoise waters of Peyto Lake, which lie 250 vertical metres (820 feet) below. However, we recommend continuing past this teeming overlook and climbing another 2.5

one of the park's most famous vistas—Peyto Lake

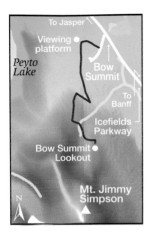

looking north from Bow Summit Lookout

kilometres (1.5 miles) to Bow Summit Lookout in search of solitude, sublime alpine meadows, and lofty views.

Beyond the viewing platform, head uphill on the right fork of two paved trails. At a three-way junction, continue on the middle branch, which angles uphill to the left of the interpretive panel. Where the paved trail turns sharply to the right, continue straight ahead on an old roadbed. The road soon switchbacks over a rise, turns southeast, and climbs steadily along the mountain slope. Wildflowers bloom in profusion along this slope in July and early August, including white-flowered valerian and white, pink, and magenta varieties of Indian paintbrush; higher up the lush growth is replaced by fields of ground-hugging white mountain avens and white and pink heather. At km 2.4 (mi 1.5) the trail drops into a basin and crosses a small stream beneath a huge rockslide —a home to marmots. A steady but brief climb beside this wall of boulders brings you to Bow Summit Lookout—a tiny alpine knoll that was once occupied by a fire lookout. From the summit, views extend north along the Mistaya Valley to Waterfowl Lakes. By following a faint, steep uphill path for another 200 metres (660 feet), you reach the best viewpoint for Bow Lake and the glaciated peaks to the south.

Peyto Lake East

Isolated shoreline on a famous lake

Length: 1.4 km (0.9 mi) one way
Elevation loss: 85 m (280 ft)
Walking time: 30 minutes one way
Starting point: Icefields Parkway, 2.4 km (1.5 mi) north of Bow Summit
Origin of the name: Bill Peyto, a local guide

SHORT HIKE

The classic, postcard view of Peyto Lake is enjoyed from the usually crowded viewpoint at Bow Summit, but on the lonely east shore of the lake you'll be all alone save for the cantankerous ghost of "Wild Bill" Peyto.

The walk to a shallow bay on the lake's east shore is short and all downhill, although the trail is not well marked. Additionally, the small, unsigned parking lot at the trailhead is easy to miss on the Icefield Parkway's downhill grade from Bow Summit (from the summit, it's on the left at

Near the lake, the forest floor is covered in moss.

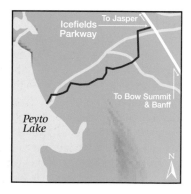

Enjoy a different perspective of this famous lake.

the top end of a long guardrail). A short, rough path leads down to the old Banff-Jasper Highway roadbed. Turn left and continue on a gradual descent of the old road for 300 metres (0.2 miles) to where an unsigned path branches left into dense forest. Another kilometre (0.6 miles) of rooty trail, muddy and mostly downhill, brings you to the lakeshore.

From the shoreline, there are dramatic views south to the Peyto Glacier and surrounding peaks, and across the lake to Caldron Peak and Mount Patterson. If you arrive on the shores of Peyto Lake in early summer, you will likely be pinned against the shore by high water levels. However, later in the season, when lake levels are lower, it is possible to walk south along a pleasant gravel beach. While you lounge on the beach, you might commune with the spirit of pioneer guide and outfitter Bill Peyto, the lake's reclusive namesake. Legend says when Peyto guided clients here at the turn of the 20th century, he would leave the "dudes" in camp on Bow Summit and hike to the lake to spend the night away from the campfire chatter.

Chephren Lake

A distinctive peak reflected in turquoise water

Length: 3.5 km (2.2 mi) one way
Elevation gain: 105 m (345 ft)
Walking time: 1 hour one way
Starting point: Waterfowl Lakes Campground, 58 km (36 mi) north along the Icefields Parkway from the Trans-Canada Hwy.
Origin of the name: The mountain's pyramid-shape suggested the tomb of the pharaoh Chephren.

SHORT HIKE

M ost travellers stop at Lower Waterfowl Lake to photograph the rugged summits of Howse Peak and Mount Chephren across it turquoise waters. Yet most do not realize an even larger lake lies in a higher basin between these two peaks or that it is an easy one-hour hike from the adjacent highway.

The trail begins at the Mistaya River footbridge at the rear of Waterfowl Lakes Campground. (If you are not registered at the campground, park at the end of the campground service road and follow a signed trail around the campground to the bridge.) After crossing the river, the trail climbs steadily through forest 1.3 kilometres (0.8 miles) to a junction. Chephren Lake is to the right, Cirque Lake (see below) to

The trail starts at this footbridge over the Mistaya River.

the left. There is little gain or loss of elevation from this junction to Chephren Lake, but the trail is often muddy. Views en route are limited to a brief glimpse of Howse Peak at a trailside meadow. After making a short descent to the lakeshore, two great peaks come into view: the

Chephren Lake

imposing, glaciated mountain to the south is Howse Peak, site of frequent avalanches in spring and early summer; Mount Chephren (pronounced "kefren") forms the west shore.

Options: Because it is a bit smaller and the approach slightly longer and steeper, **Cirque Lake** is less frequently visited than Chephren. From the junction 1.3 kilometres (0.8 miles) from the main trailhead, the Cirque Lake trail spurs southwest (left), quickly reaching the lake's outlet stream, then climbing beside it through heavy subalpine forest to the lake. If you visit both lakes, the total round trip distance is 12.8 kilometres (eight miles) and you should allow four hours.

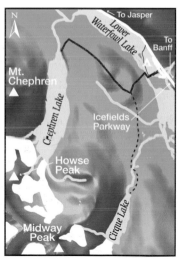

Warden Lake

A peaceful lake where crowds are nonexistent

Length: 2.2 km (1.4 mi) one way
Elevation gain: 30 m (100 ft)
Walking time: 40 minutes one way
Starting point: Warden station, along the Icefields Parkway 2 km (1.2 mi) south of Saskatchewan River Crossing. (Park on the gravel road opposite the warden station and look for the small trail sign on the highway just south of the warden station)
Origin of the name: A favourite destination for park staff based at the nearby warden station

SHORT HIKE

Once you are clear of the Saskatchewan River Crossing Warden Station and the sounds of the Icefields Parkway, the short, flat walk to Warden Lake is pure joy. Walking alongside the North Saskatchewan River and looking back to the Continental Divide, you could almost believe you are in the wilds of the Yukon. And the small,

For much of its way, the trail to Warden Lake follows the North Saskatchewan River.

quiet lake at trail's end is seldom visited except by waterfowl, moose, and black bear.

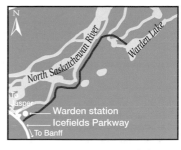

The trail begins by skirting along the south side of the warden station and its horse corral, then traverses rocky spruce flats to come abreast of the North Saskatchewan River on an old roadbed. The wide trail continues beside the river for nearly one kilometre (0.6 miles), with sweeping views across the braided river to Mount Wilson. It then breaks away to the right along a marshy meadow and disappears into the forest as a single-track trail. At km 1.9 (mi 1.1), a small forest-enclosed pond is reached. The trail then climbs through the forest and suddenly the wide expanse of Warden Lake comes into view. For wardens and other park staff based at Saskatchewan River Crossing, the lake is a popular spot for an evening walk or paddle. Across its waters to the south, Mount Murchison rises like a giant castle—little wonder natives thought it the highest mountain in the Rockies since its summit stands nearly two vertical kilometres (well over a mile) above the valley floor.

Warden Lake

Howse River Viewpoint

Following in the footsteps of history

Length: 2.3 km (1.4 mi) one way
Elevation gain: 50 m (160 ft), elevation loss 80 m (260 ft)
Walking time: 40 minutes one way
Starting point: Icefields Parkway, 3 km (1.9 mi) north of Saskatchewan River Crossing
Origin of the name: Fur trader Joseph Howse, who crossed the Canadian Rockies in 1810

SHORT HIKE

Officially, it is the trail to Glacier Lake, which is a fairly strenuous full-day or overnight trip. But you can take a 40-minute walk along this trail to a panoramic viewpoint overlooking the Howse River, which was the route used by fur traders to reach the Columbia River in the early 1800s.

The trail to the viewpoint begins by leading through a forest of lodgepole pine. Near the end of the first kilometre (0.6 mile), the trail

crossing the North Saskatchewan River

descends to the North Saskatchewan River, which is crossed on a deluxe footbridge. The river here funnels through a short canyon, a worthwhile destination in itself. After climbing from the gorge, there is more relatively flat, forested walking until the trail reaches an

the panorama from Howse River Viewpoint

open ridge. From here, Howse River Viewpoint is across a grassy bluff to the left. Stroll along this ridge from the main trail to soak up the vista extending up-valley toward Howse Pass. Despite being so near the busy Icefields Parkway, you will experience a real sense of remote wilderness in this locale where David Thompson camped for two weeks during his historic first crossing of the Rockies in 1807. (Read about the journey and that of Joseph Howse on interpretive boards at the roadside pullout south of The Crossing Resort.)

Options: For fit and enthusiastic hikers, it is possible to reach and return from **Glacier Lake** in one day. From the Howse River Viewpoint, the trail descends to braided flats along the Howse River then cuts inland and crosses a forested ridge to Glacier Lake. With a spectacular backdrop of glaciated peaks, the three-kilometre-long (1.9-mile) lake is a worthy destination. Total roundtrip from the Icefields Parkway is 18 kilometres (11.1 miles), for which six hours should be allowed.

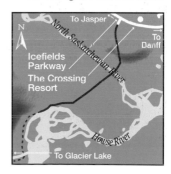

[1] signposted as Glacier Lake

Parker Ridge

Sweeping glacier views from an alpine meadow

Length: 2.7 km (1.7 mi) one way
Elevation gain: 250 m (820 ft)
Walking time: 1 hour one way
Starting point: 41 km (25 mi) north along the Icefields Parkway from Saskatchewan River Crossing and 4 km (2.5 mi) south of park boundary
Origin of the name: Herschel C. Parker, who began a survey of The Continental Divide in 1897

SHORT HIKE

Saskatchewan Glacier from Parker Ridge

One of the finest short trails in Banff National Park switchbacks up to a treeless 2,250-metre-high (7,380-foot) ridge where views stretch to the longest glacier extending from the Columbia Icefield. The hike up should take an hour or less, and along the way you will discover many of the plants and wildlife of the alpine world.

For the first one kilometre (0.6 miles), the trail climbs across avalanche paths and past stands of stunted alpine fir. Wildflowers are particularly lush and showy here, well-watered by a melting snowpack that lingers well into July. At an elevation of around 2,100 metres (6,800 feet), the trail switchbacks above the last stunted trees and emerges into the alpine zone, where ground-hugging wildflowers like moss campion, white mountain avens, rock jasmine and forget-me-nots survive in a desert-like, wind-blasted landscape. Nearing the crest of the ridge, you pass through rocky terrain inhabited by pikas. The steady uphill slog ends after 2.1 kilometres (1.3 miles), as the trail crosses the summit and angles left to viewpoints for the Saskatchewan Glacier. This nine-kilometre-long (5.6-mile) tongue of ice dwarfs in size the nearby, tourist-swarmed Athabasca Glacier, and the peaks and waterfalls rising from the valley are wild and impressive. Scan the meadows and openings in the scattered forest beneath the viewpoint since the area is frequently visited by mountain goats and, sometimes, grizzly bears.

Trees along Parker Ridge stunted by harsh weather conditions are known as krummholz, a German word meaning "twisted wood."

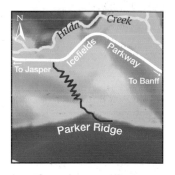

Note: To help preserve the fragile meadows, Parks Canada usually keeps Parker Ridge closed until the trail is snowfree. Therefore, you should check on the status at a park visitor centre if you plan on hiking it before mid-July.

Helen Lake

The tranquility of an alpine lake

Length: 6 km (3.7 mi) one way
Elevation gain: 450 m (1,480 ft)
Walking time: 2 hours one way
Starting point: 33 km (20.5 mi) north along the Icefields Parkway from the Trans-Canada Hwy. (opposite Crowfoot Glacier Viewpoint)
Origin of the name: The daughter of American Alpine Club member Reverend H.P. Nichols

DAY TRIP

Wildflower meadows, lofty lakes and castellate peaks provide a constant change of scene that will draw you onward to a remarkable panorama of a vast, alpine landscape.

From the Icefields Parkway, this trail climbs steadily through forest along the west-facing slopes of the Bow Valley for three kilometres (1.9

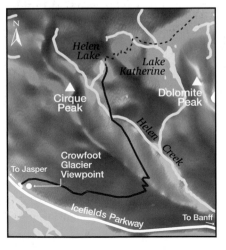

miles), before emerging onto steep mountainside meadows. Views open across the valley to Crowfoot Mountain and Glacier, and the sharp summit of Mount Hector to the southeast. The trail reaches the south end of a long ridge at km 3.4 (mi 2.1), where it switches 180 degrees and contours into the amphitheatre containing Helen Lake. After another one kilometre

(0.6 miles) of gradual ascent through lightly forested meadows, it descends to the base of a rockslide surrounded by a lush snow-bed plant community containing an amazing profusion of subalpine wildflowers. Beyond the slide, the trail climbs above the last trees and stays above treeline for the remainder of the way.

Helen Lake is bordered by open alpine meadows and scree slopes beneath the summit of Cirque Peak. It is a great place to kick back and enjoy the scene, which is animated by the antics of the resident hoary marmots, who seem to have nothing better to do than sit in the sun and count passing hikers.

Helen Lake

Options: Helen Lake would be an above average destination on most hikes, but you shouldn't end your day there. Gather your strength and continue for 900 metres (0.6 miles) up a series of steep switchbacks to a rocky ridge that provides an outstanding view of **Katherine Lake** and **Dolomite Pass** to the east and Helen Lake and its meadows back to the southwest.

Nigel Pass

Views of the remote north

Length: 7.2 km (4.5 mi) one way
Elevation gain: 335 m (1,100 ft)
Walking time: 2 to 2.5 hours one way
Starting point: 36.5 km (23 mi) north along the Icefields Parkway from Saskatchewan River Crossing and 8.5 km (5.5 mi) south of the park boundary
Origin of the name: Nigel Vavasour, a packer for an early climbing expedition

DAY TRIP

Nigel Creek is your constant companion

Nigel Pass is one of the most rewarding day trips in the north end of the park. Atop this open, rocky ridge on the boundary of Banff and Jasper National Parks, hikers are rewarded with expansive views back to rugged, glaciated peaks near the Columbia Icefield and north into the remote Brazeau River Valley.

From beyond the locked gate at the parking area, the trail branches right off the gravel roadbed, crosses Nigel Creek, and then contours across avalanche paths above the creek. After two kilometers (1.2 miles), it reaches a campsite used by native hunters, mountaineer-explorers, and the early Banff-Jasper Highway motorists (look for carvings made by these visitors on the surrounding trees). At this point, the trail veers north and begins its ascent of the upper Nigel Creek Valley. Throughout this section there are good views back to Parker Ridge and Hilda Peak (a sharp sub-peak of Mount Athabasca), while Nigel Pass is seldom out of sight ahead. The trail climbs more seriously over the final one kilometre (0.6 miles) to the pass, which is reached where a cairn marks the boundary between Banff and Jasper National Parks. Forest cover is sparse and stunted on this 2,195-metre-high (7,200-foot) ridge, but unimpeded views extend back to the south as far as the ice-clad summit of Mount Saskatchewan rising beyond Parker Ridge.

wildflowers just before the pass

Options: It takes just a short descent beyond Nigel Pass to reach the **Brazeau River** (an easy rock-hop crossing). A trail continues downstream along a rocky slope for another kilometre or so (less than a mile) to a large, marshy meadow, a rock wall featuring several small waterfalls, and views of the Brazeau River Valley and the maze of peaks comprising the southern region of Jasper National Park. A longer option is to head upstream along the dwindling Brazeau River approximately four kilometres (2.5 miles) to its headwaters in a small lake beneath **Cataract Pass**.

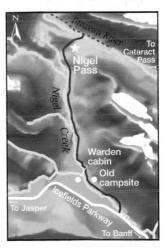

[1] signposted as Nigel Creek

Sources

Banff Lake Louise Tourism

Website: www.banfflakelouise.com
The website of this marketing organization is a good source of practical information to help plan your trip to Banff National Park.

Banff Visitor Centre

224 Banff Avenue, Banff
Phone: (403) 762-1550
The main source of information for visitors once they arrive in the park. Combines a Parks Canada information desk, information from the local tourism association, a theatre, and a retail outlet.

Friends of Banff National Park

Phone (403) 762-8918
Website: www.friendsofbanff.com
Non-profit organization selling books and maps specific to Banff National Park. Retail outlets located in the Banff Visitor Centre (224 Banff Ave.) and The Bear and the Butterfly (214 Banff Ave.).

Gem Trek Publishing

Website: www.gemtrek.com
This company produces maps for all regions of the Canadian Rockies. Relief shading shows elevation, and all hiking trails have been plotted using a global positioning system.

Lake Louise Visitor Centre

Samson Mall, Lake Louise
Phone: (403) 522-3833
An information desk and natural history displays in the village of Lake Louise.

Parks Canada

Website: www.pc.gc.ca
The government agency that manages Canada's national parks and national historic sites. Website has details on each park and historic site, including information on fees, campgrounds, and wildlife.

Town of Banff

Phone: 403 762-1200
Website: www.banff.ca
To many people's surprise, the town of Banff is a bustling community of 8,000 permanent residents.

Travel Alberta

Phone: (780) 427-4321 or (800) 252-3782
Website: www.travelalberta.com
The marketing organization responsible for promoting tourism in Alberta to the world.

Whyte Museum of the Canadian Rockies

111 Bear Street, Banff
Phone: (403) 762-2291
Website: www.whyte.org
Preserves the human and cultural history of the Canadian Rockies.

Alpine Club of Canada
Phone: (403) 678-3200
Website: www.alpineclubofcanada.ca
Operates a network of remote back-country alpine huts throughout the Canadian Rockies, including seven in Banff National Park.

Hostelling International—Canada
Phone: (613) 237-7884
Website: www.hihostels.ca
Operates five hostels within Banff National Park, including in the town of Banff and Lake Louise.

Parks Canada Campground Reservation Service
Phone: (877) 737-3783
Website: www.pccamping.ca
An online reservation service that includes the most popular campgrounds in Banff National Park.

Shadow Lake Lodge
Phone: (403) 762-0116 or
(866) 762-0114
Website: www.shadowlakelodge.com
See page 84 for a description of the hiking trail leading to this backcountry lodge.

Skoki Lodge
Phone: (877) 822-7669
Website: www.skoki.com
See page 112 for a description of the hiking trail leading to this backcountry lodge.

White Mountain Adventures
Phone: (403) 762 7889 or
(800) 408-0005
Website:
www.sunshinemeadowsbanff.com
Provides shuttle bus service to Sunshine Meadows (see page 72).

Banff Gondola web-cam
Website: www.banffgondola.com
Click on the link at this website to see live pictures of the weather around the town of Banff.

Environment Canada Weather Office
Phone: (403) 762-2088
Website: www.weatheroffice.gc.ca
Weather phone provides recorded conditions and forecasts that are updated throughout the day. The website displays weather maps and forecasts for specific communities across Canada, including the town of Banff.

Ambulance
Phone: **911** or (403) 762-2222

Banff Fire Station
Phone: **911** or (403) 762-1250

Lake Louise Medical Clinic
Phone: (403) 522-2184

Mineral Springs Hospital (Banff)
Phone: (403) 762-2222

RCMP
Phone: **911** or (403) 762-2226

Warden Office
Phone: (403) 762-1470

Index